What people are saying . . .

In *Victory through Light: How to Overcome the Growing Cultural Darkness* Victoria Dorshorn confronts the "darkness that is growing in our culture today" through the light of God's Word. This is not a quick and easy read. Rather, it is a book to thoughtfully and prayerfully study. I especially recommend it as a resource for small groups and Sunday school classes.
  —Marlene Bagnull, Author, Speaker, and Director of Write His Answer Ministries

Victory through Light takes a very thoughtful and well-researched look at our contemporary Western world with equally thoughtful biblical responses and practical questions for reflection and response.
  —Peter Lundell, D. Miss., Author, Pastor, and Teacher

Victory through Light boldly addresses contemporary issues from a Biblical perspective, offering Scriptural justification for the author's assertions and ultimate conclusions. She tackles sensitive subjects, such as homosexuality, abortion, illicit sex, evolution, and cultural darkness skillfully, in a "politically incorrect" manner. She sheds light on the pervasive religion of tolerance, the erosion of truth and the prevalence of moral relativism that destroys objective morality and absolute Truth, refuting the lies of human philosophies with Scripture and rejecting the acceptance and celebration of sin. The author believes the devaluation of life through abortion emanates from a deep disrespect for God as Creator. A thread of hope permeates the book, leading the reader from the dark pit of despair to the True Light of Christ that triumphs over darkness.

For the serious Bible student, Victoria offers thought-provoking and challenging discussion questions at the end of each chapter. Scriptures, Endnotes, and Bibliography provide additional resources.

I highly recommend this book as a study tool, as its content and style are suitable for new and mature Christians, as well as Bible school and seminary students.

—Angie B. Williams, Pastor, Author, and Public Speaker

In *Victory through Light: How to Overcome the Growing Cultural Darkness*, Victoria Dorshorn exposes the darkness that has descended over American culture. As she explains, it's not as much an invading force as one that's been invited in. Through the acceptance of various assumptions and theories about life and death, meaning and truth, origins and destiny, American culture has increasingly opted for an anti-Christian, unbiblical, and immoral approach to living and governing. Consequently, what was once thought good is now evil, and what was once thought false is now true. This is the darkness Dorshorn exposes as she also points us back to the Light—Jesus the Christ and his way. We need to understand the darkness, and Dorshorn helps with that. But we also need to find our way back to the Light, and Dorshorn shows us the way and shares with us what we will find there. This book is important. Read it. Digest it. Apply it.

—William D. Watkins, Award-winning Author, Editor, and President of Literary Solutions

This is a book that just had to be written. In *Victory through Light*, Victoria Dorshorn has not only given clarity to the age-old problem of many—that of discerning the Light of Christ from the false "lights" of this world; she also gives us a catalog of very real and practical responses to the Light of the World. Victoria Dorshorn not only exhorts us *to* live in the light, she tells us *how* we can live in the light.

—Rev. Michael Gantt, Author, Speaker, Missionary, and Executive Director of the Kenya Development Fund

Victory through Light by Victoria Dorshorn is a timely, must- and easy-to-read narrative exposing the nonsense of relativism that our culture and, unfortunately, many churches adopt, embrace, and promote. As this condition becomes normalized, any other point of view is violently rejected.

Ms. Dorshorn's work is very convicting to me as a believer and follower of Jesus Christ. Where have I made compromises of God's truth and His commandments for living a life of moral excellence? For example, as I watch the persecution (not prosecution) of our duly elected president, I have used choice language regarding several Democrats and especially the Speaker of the House. Unfortunately, each day provides me new opportunities to practice Philippians 4:4-8.

Ms. Dorshorn does not pull any punches. When challenging our culture's attitude regarding truth, she states, "This creates a conundrum, for if every person's truth is true, and my truth says that not every person's truth is true, then it must be accepted as true that not all truths are true. Talk about mental chaos and social disruption." So, if one is willing to address the discussion questions and personal reflection issues at the end of each chapter, I'm confident *Victory through Light* will stimulate a closer relationship with Jesus our Creator under His governance, to the Glory of God our Father.

—Charles J. Patricoff, Author and Conference Speaker

As we look around in our culture today and see the moral decay that is taking place, we can feel the powers of this world working overtime. In *Victory through Light*, Victoria Dorshorn uses illustrations, personal stories, and, most importantly, Scripture, to shed light into the darkness.

—Anita McKee, Women's Bible Study Leader and Youth Teacher

There are those things in life we would rather ignore and pretend aren't really taking place around us. *Victory through Light* will push you to look at them head on and will give you biblical advice on how to fight against them.

—Rachael Collins, Author, Speaker, and Lay Minister at United Wesleyan Church, Easley, SC

In *Victory through Light*, Victoria Dorshorn presents a very practical yet challenging approach that helps her readers examine what is truly influencing their lives. This book expounds the truth of God's Word beautifully! It also gives the reader an opportunity through personal reflection to seek God for the heart change that only He provides. Victoria points the way to saving faith in the One and only Savior, Jesus Christ. This book will lead you to think critically about our culture and your place in it.

—Jody Beckham, Master's Student at Midwestern Baptist Theological Seminary

Victory through Light

How to Overcome the Growing Cultural Darkness

Victoria Dorshorn

Victory Publishing
Baldwin City, Kansas

© 2020 by Victoria Dorshorn

Published by Victory Publishing
Baldwin City, KS 66006

All rights reserved. No part of this publication may be reproduced, stored in a retrieval system, or transmitted in any form or by any means—for example, electronic, photocopy, recording—without the prior written permission of Victory Publishing, 392 E. 900th Rd, Baldwin City, KS 66006, or of the author at victoria@carrolldorshorn.com. The only exception is brief quotations in printed or online reviews, or as by provided by USA copyright law.

Library of Congress Control Number: 2020901708
ISBN: 978-1-7345393-0-1 (softcover)

This title is also available as an electronic book, available from major outlets.

All Scripture quotations, unless otherwise indicated, are taken from *The Holy Bible, King James Version*, KJV.

Scripture marked MEV® is taken from the *Modern English Version*. Copyright © 2014 by Military Bible Association. Used by permission. All rights reserved.

Scripture marked NKJV® is taken from *The Nelson Study Bible: New King James Version*. Copyright © 1997 by Thomas Nelson, Inc. New King James Version®. Copyright © 1979, 1980, 1982 by Thomas Nelson, Inc. Used by permission. All rights reserved.

Scripture from *The Interlinear Bible*, including the Hebrew-Aramaic Old Testament and the Greek-English New Testament, 2nd ed., © 1985 by Jay P. Green, Sr., published by Hendrickson Publishers, Peabody, Massachusetts is used by permission. All rights reserved.

Copy Editing, Proofreading, and Cover Design: Marlene Bagnull

Cover photo: Muka In Room

Author Photo: Sarah Reynolds

Printed in the United States of America

First edition: 10 9 8 7 6 5 4 3 2 1

For Chuck and Betty Fuller, who taught me much

✝

"And the things that thou hast heard of me among many witnesses, the same commit thou to faithful men, who shall be able to teach others also."
—2 Timothy 2:2

Contents

Acknowledgments 11

Introduction 13

Encroaching Darkness 15

Darkness for Light 21

Disappearing Light 31

Dark Origins... 43

Day of Darkness 57

Absence of Light.. 67

Works of Darkness 77

Artificial Lights 93

The False Light 111

The True Light 123

Children of Light... 133

Triumph of Light... 149

Endnotes 163

Bibliography 171

Suggested Reading... 175

About the Author 177

Acknowledgments

I thank my husband, without whose love and patience I could not have completed this project. I thank my family, friends, and writing associates for their reassurance along the way.

A special thanks to Marlene Bagnull, who went above and beyond with editing advice, encouragement, and help. When I felt like giving up, she was there with timely Scriptures and helpful suggestions. Her endorsement renewed my resolve to complete the publishing process.

Also, a special thanks to all who were kind enough to read the book and provide feedback and endorsements, including Peter Lundell, Angie Williams, William Watkins, and Michael Gantt, as well as others.

A special thanks to Charles and Mary Patricoff who read an early version of the book and gave such positive feedback as to propel me forward. From the beginning, Charles's exhortation to me was to "get this book done."

A big thanks to my other beta readers, Charles and Anita McKee, Gerald and Ruth Clock, Tessa Chipman, Jody Beckham, and Rachael Collins. Your encouragement kept me on track.

And, of course, I thank the Lord Jesus, who is my inspiration and Light. Without him, I can do nothing. In him, I can do all things.

Introduction

You will notice headings for "Discussion Questions," "Personal Reflection," and "Verses to Consider" at the end of each chapter. These may be answered individually or in group studies. To limit the cost of the book, I haven't left space in the text for your answers.

However, it is my hope that completing these exercises will take you deeper into the gospel and will enrich your spiritual walk with the Lord. You might purchase a spiral notebook and track your progress in that—much more cost effective than having to purchase a separate workbook. The main thing is that you "grow in grace, and in the knowledge of our Lord and Savior Jesus Christ" (2 Peter 3:18).

And if you haven't made a commitment to Christ yet, my prayer is that you will before you finish this book.

In any event, may you be enlightened, encouraged, and empowered by the True Light, Jesus, and by his Word. May his love envelope you and enable you to love others. And may you experience and enjoy victory through light as you overcome the growing cultural darkness.

This then is the message which we have heard of him,
and declare unto you, that God is light,
and in him is no darkness at all. 1 John 1:5

[God] . . . has called you out of darkness into
his marvelous light. 1 Peter 2:9

CHAPTER 1

†

Encroaching Darkness

LET US PRETEND . . .

You're strolling around your neighborhood as evening falls. You've taken this walk many times before. But this time something is strangely different. As the shadows deepen, you have an increasing sense of insecurity. The gray areas seem to fade to darker gray; the darker gray shadows blacken. You want to run, but you can't see clearly enough to move that fast. You step from shadow to shadow into a growing darkness. You lose sight of familiar landmarks, houses of people you know, trees that you have rested under before, when the sky was brighter.

Your heart rate speeds. You break out in a sweat. Breaths come fast and shallow.

You see no lights in the windows. No streetlamps come on. Why is the darkness advancing like this? Where are the familiar pathways? What sound do you hear besides the pounding of your heart? The sound of someone—or something—stalking you?

Maybe it's the echo of your own footsteps that frightens you. The sound grows closer. Maybe there is someone following you, someone lurking in the shadows to grab you, someone waiting ahead to pounce upon you. You can't be sure. Heart racing, you move forward. You bump into a wall, so you inch your way along whatever wall that is, feeling your way with your fingertips. Sight is all but gone. Terror grips you.

You can't be sure of anything. That uncertainty envelopes you in a hazy fog, and fear enfolds you like a dark shroud. In these last moments, what started out as a nice walk through familiar territory has become this nightmare from which you cannot awaken.

And now the wall ends. There's nothing left to hang onto. You can't even walk by feeling your way now. You can't see. You stand, frozen to the spot, terrified of the enemies in the darkness. They might be imagined. But they might be real.

You try to take a step forward, but it seems that there is no ground for your foot to touch. Are you at the edge of a precipice? Or is that just the curb of the street?

You scream, not really expecting help but to release fear; but the sound of your own voice intensifies your terror. You stiffen, expecting unseen enemies to pounce. Surely death awaits.

You see a glimmer of light like a single firefly on an overcast night of new moon. It moves toward you, growing brighter as it comes. By its light you can see the ugliness of the things that surround you. You recoil from them, but at the same time, the light reveals your place in those things.

As the light nears and reveals more, you squeeze your eyes to quench it, to restore the darkness, which has become comforting. The brighter the light glows, the more you turn from it, blocking it out of your vision. Yes, the darkness is fearful, but the light pierces your soul, convicts you of necessary change. You turn your back on the light.

Encroaching Darkness

When you look down, you see the dark street gutter open up to an unfathomable, dark hole. No light shines there at all. After one glance back at the advancing light, you step into the dark pit below.

You become aware of falling, in slow motion, down, down, down, into the blackness. And now it surrounds you. But you can feel something under your feet, some kind of solid ground that keeps you from plummeting to the depths of this pit.

You glance up, but there is no light visible. The darkness squeezes in on you, and you realize you can't get out of this place into which you have descended. You are surrounded by darkness. You try to climb out but there is nowhere to grasp or get a foothold. And when you step off the little foundation, there is nothing. You must keep your feet right where they are or lose all sense of standing on solid ground.

The darkness settles upon you like a mist, and you know you are in the land of darkness. The black shadow of death is around you. Will this last forever? You pinch yourself. You feel it. No dream. Is this what dying feels like? Are you even alive?

You hear moaning and wheezing around you and smell the stench of stale mold and rotting meat. "Give me light," you plead.

Your only answer is your own mind recalling words you once heard: "The eye is the lamp of the body. Therefore when your eye is good, your whole body also is full of light. But when your eye is bad, your body also is full of darkness. Take heed therefore lest the light which is in you is darkness" (Luke 11:34-35 MEV).

How did you remember those words? And why, now, would they come to mind? What do they mean?

You rub your eyes, blink, and blink again. Nothing changes.

You begin to hyperventilate, magnifying the horrid smells around you. Your lungs feel as though they are filling with liquid darkness. You scream, but only air comes out. How did you get here?

Again, your mind whispers words you didn't know you knew: "This is the verdict, that light has come into the world, and men loved darkness rather than light, because their deeds were evil. For everyone who does evil hates the light and does not come to the light, lest his deeds should be exposed. But he who does the truth comes to the light, that it may be revealed that his deeds have been done in God" (John 3:19-21 MEV).

In your heart, you know the words are true, even though you don't remember ever memorizing them or paying much attention to them at all.

From above you comes a tender voice: "I have called you out of darkness into my light."

You reach a hand up, as though you believe a hand will reach down to you to lift you out. "Who are you?" you manage to ask, your voice weak and squeaky. But there is nothing there except a glimmer of light so far away you can't even estimate the distance.

The voice speaks again, "Awake, you who sleep, arise from the dead, and Christ will give you light" (Eph. 5:14 MEV).

You stretch both arms up, though your mind tells you to be strong in yourself, to not give in to such foolishness. You intuitively realize that this is the most important decision in your life. You can call for deliverance, or you can cling to the darkness wherein you may do as you please. Or so you assume. Keep your arms raised for help or drop them and plunge deeper into this inescapable darkness.

You know that if you choose the darkness, you will float in this pit forever. Are you okay with that?

Light or darkness. Your choice. This could be your last invitation out of darkness into light. But do you prefer the presumed secrecy of darkness?

Discussion Questions

1. What did this story mean to you?

2. What kinds of spiritual darkness could it be representing?

3. Discuss a time when you needed someone else to cast light upon your life.

4. Discuss a time when God enabled you to be light for someone else. What were the results?

Personal Reflection

1. Think of a time when you felt that you were in darkness. This can be spiritual, mental, or emotional. It can be depression, hopelessness, or confusion. Did you look for light? Or were you content to remain in that state? Be honest with yourself and with the Lord.

2. Do you know someone who is lost in the darkness of our culture? Do you think that you can throw them a lifeline or be a light for them?

3. Read John 1:6-9 and 3:19-21. Is the True Light that came into the world a person? Who is that person? These verses declare that he is the Son of God, Jesus Christ. Have you already come to his light? Do you want to come to dwell in his light?

Verses to Consider

1. Read John 8:12, 32, 36; 12:46; and 14:6; 1 John 1:5; and Philippians 2:14-16.

    (a) Is there any darkness at all in God?

    (b) Since Jesus is the True Light, if we belong to Jesus, are we then light?

(c) If we are light, do we have a responsibility to shine light into a dark world?

2. Read Luke 11:33-36. Jesus speaks figuratively here, using the eye as a symbol of what a person focuses on. If a person focuses on what is true and good—the Light of Jesus, then that person's life will radiate light to others. If a person focuses on what is deceptive and evil—the darkness of the pit and its source of darkness (discussed in later chapters), then that person's life will be full of darkness.

(a) If there is no darkness in God and if we are to have no darkness in us, what relationship with God do we need? Faith in him or rebellion from him?

(b) Do you want to be light to others?

(c) List some things you can do to be a light to others. Try to think of specific situations.

CHAPTER 2

†

Darkness for Light

GROWING UP A TREKKIE, I found myself surprised when I enjoyed the *Transformer* movies, as my grandson introduced me to them. I liked the Autobots, of course. Especially Bumblebee. I was like a kid at Universal Studios when I discovered the real Bumblebee in the Prop House. That was a selfie I had to take, but since he was sooooo tall, I had to have another visitor snap the picture to get him all in as he towered above me. And I looked very tiny. (Now Bumblebee has his own movie, released in December of 2018.)

On a different trip, I encountered a life-size Iron Man. Got that picture too and showed it to a child at church, not knowing that Iron Man was his hero. His alter ego, in fact. You can imagine the response I received.

Quite frankly, I was shocked, having missed a whole generation of superheroes. I didn't understand much about Transformers when my children were collecting them in the 80s, though I remembered Superman from my childhood, along with Zorro and the Lone Ranger. It seems superheroes have multiplied since the 50s. But what do they all have in common? Traditional superheroes seek the triumph of good over evil. In fact, most movies include a struggle of good and evil. And there's the conundrum . . . .

When we say "good over evil," we assume that there is a "good" and an "evil," and that there's a discernable difference between the two. Not everything is good. Some things are evil. Philosophers have wrestled with this question for ages. Literally. And all religions hinge on our discernment between the two. There must be an objective moral law or principle which enables us to judge between good behavior and bad behavior, a standard that tells us which is which. Otherwise, behavior is subjective, and the standard constantly changing.

Moreover, if we accept a standard, an objective moral law, we must also accept a moral lawgiver, because if there isn't a moral lawgiver, then anyone can set or change the standard, and it would be no longer a moral law. Ravi Zacharias states this succinctly in his book *The End of Reason*:

- When you assert that there is such a thing as evil, you must assume there is such a thing as good.

- When you say there is such a thing as good, you must assume there is a moral law by which to distinguish between good and evil. There must be some standard by which to determine what is good and what is evil.

- When you assume a moral law, you must posit a moral lawgiver—the source of the moral law.[1]

Thus, any time we expect good to triumph over evil, or even suspect that evil is winning over good, we must also accept the reality and presence of a moral lawgiver, one who defines what is good and what is evil.

This book takes the position that the Judeo-Christian God is that lawgiver. Otherwise, who gets to determine what is good or evil? As Ravi Zacharias often says in his speeches, "In some cultures they love their neighbors; in other cultures they eat them. Which do you prefer?"

If we let different cultures or groups in a culture determine what is good or evil, we end up in confusion.

And try as they might, the postmodern relativists cannot obliterate these distinctions, even with their mantras of "true for you but not for me," "whatever you think is right is right for you," and "there is no evil or good; it's a matter of personal choice." Being blatant denials of reality, these ideas give power and permission to the rapist, serial killer, kidnapper, and terrorist. They enable the identity thief, bank robber, and common burglar.

Thus, with even moviemakers acknowledging the reality of good and evil, enter Bumblebee and other Autobots to defeat the Decepticons; and enter Iron Man and other superheroes to set things right. But that's only in the world of fiction. As they say, "Only in the movies."

What about the real world? Who gets to set things right here in reality? Jesus Christ, the Son of the Living God. He defeated evil when he died on the cross. Through his resurrection, he gave us the ability to refuse evil. He brings love, peace, joy, hope, comfort, true righteousness, grace, and life abundant and eternal. He is and brings light that shatters the darkness. But how? Keep reading.

While it's not likely that an evening walk, as described in Chapter 1, would turn out like that in reality, we may sometimes feel that we have ended up in the deepening shadows of a spiritual, emotional, or mental realm. And no wonder, given the present cultural norms of our society. With the entertainment industry and media saturating us with relative morality, situational ethics, and the removal of absolute moral truth, we may find it easy to compromise what we know to be truth and spiritual light.

In fact, secular Hollywood has begun making the "good" superheroes actually be the villains. They have given superpowers to evil anti-heroes, making them appear desirable and enviable. Some of their children's movies are nothing more than propaganda tools for the immoral left. But the movies make it look so good . . . just a little shade of gray perhaps . . . surely, they must be right.

Just think for a moment what you saw on television last night. Just last night. Now, think back to what you've seen in the past week.

No, I'm not going to say, "Don't watch TV or movies." They can be a wonderful source of entertainment. However, when I find myself rooting for the good guy to hurry up and kill the bad guy to save the system the cost of a trial and to ensure that the criminal doesn't "walk" on a technicality, I have to ask myself, "What am I thinking?"

It was easy to root for Carl Lee Hailey (played by Samuel L. Jackson) in *A Time to Kill*, because his ten-year-old daughter, Tanya, had been brutally raped and injured for life by two young, white racists who likely would have been acquitted in the Mississippi Delta in the 1980s. Hailey kills the young men before they go to trial. When the KKK rises up, the audience cheers their demise and rejoices when Hailey is cleared of all charges. His white attorney brings his own daughter over to play with Tonya, leaving us with a feel-good attitude about the much needed end to racism.

The movie was based on the John Grisham novel of the same title, itself a riveting story. But would the same end have been reached if the father had not killed the perpetrators, but instead the trial had been of the two racists—and they, of necessity, were found guilty? Would that have been believable? This movie makes a good case for situational ethics and relative morality. And there the darkness begins.

Many viewers found it easy to accept Paul Kersey's relentless revenge on gang members in the series of 1970 movies starring Charles Bronson, the *Death Wish* series. This series, above all others, seemed to usher in the acceptability of revenge killing—at least in the movies.

It's not a bad thing to want to see the scales of justice tipped in favor of the good person who is horribly wronged by the bad person. But situational ethics, relative morality, or whatever else we might call it, is dangerous. It is dangerous to the individual, to the family, and to society. It is dangerous because once we blur the lines between good and evil, right and wrong, we lose safe boundaries.

Once we accept gray areas as normal, expected, and dominant, we are left with a multitude of shades of gray. And once everything becomes "just another shade of gray," it is easy to slip into the darkness, to call good evil and evil good. It is dangerous because such relevance spreads to other areas of life, injuring the innocent, destroying relationships, and defiling the culture.

Our society has programmed us for this compromise. In addition to the entertainment and media industries, our public educational system, as well as higher education, all too eagerly has rushed down this path. One has only to look at the reading material in middle schools to see how the stories forced upon our children and grandchildren are secular propaganda (and often atheistic). Moreover, political correctness and a redefined tolerance are the new laws by which society tells us to live. If we look to the past and to the Bible, we see that the prophet Isaiah wrote, "Woe unto them that call evil good, and good evil; that put darkness for light, and light for darkness; that put bitter for sweet, and sweet for bitter" (Isa. 5:20). That's exactly what is happening in our culture today. And the result will be "woe."

I have seen a certain quotation attributed both to Booker T. Washington and to Rick Warren. It's possible that Rick Warren quoted Booker T. Washington, and the person who attributed the quote to Warren didn't catch the citation. At any rate, it's a wise statement: "A lie doesn't become truth, wrong doesn't become right, and evil doesn't become good, just because it's accepted by a majority." I might revise that to say, "just because a warped culture of political correctness says so."

Victory through Light

Whew! This is heavy, huh? And yet, who among us has never been convinced that a certain action, attitude, or behavior was *relatively* right, even though we knew in our heart that others would disagree, and that even the Bible would contradict our decision? But our minds were conditioned to yield to natural urges and reasoning so that we could justify our choice.

There have been people in my life who have done so. There have been times in my life when I have been deceived (or deceived myself) into taking a course of action which I knew was contrary to the Word of God and to my faith. If we're honest, we all can admit to compromising, however slightly, even if it's just validating activities which we know are wrong. Studies show us that 61% of single Christians are okay with casual sex and that only 11% of self-identified Christians think that sex should be reserved only for marriage.[2] That's just one example of the eroded morality of our time.

We may argue that ours is a special situation . . . a gift from God . . . a special but secret ministry . . . and so on . . . but once we start down that road, look out. The darkness closes in fast. The walls and fences disappear. We can't even continue to walk by feeling our way. We fall into a dark pit and plunge downward. Not literally, of course, but figuratively. Spiritually. It's not that we lose salvation if we are born again, but that we lose our way. We lose the presence of our light.

And our present culture helps us head down this path. Evil doesn't show up boldly and proclaim itself as evil. It sneaks in, under the guise of being good. Former Literature Professor and Provost at Patrick Henry College, Gene Edward Veith writes, "Evil associates itself with a noble cause or with high-sounding words. Abortion associates itself with the emancipation of women. Illicit sex associates itself with love. . . . Thus, even manifest sinners cling steadfastly to their own righteousness."[3] Indeed, when we call evil "good" and good "evil," perversion runs rampant and self-righteousness reigns.

However, all is not doom and gloom. There is hope. There is peace. There is love. There is forgiveness. There is redemption and reconciliation. There is light in the shadows, waiting and longing to show up and shatter the darkness for us, to set us free. See 1 John 1:8-2:2. My paraphrase of the KJV passage follows.

> If we say that we have no sin, we deceive ourselves, and we are not telling the truth. If we confess our sins, God is faithful and just to forgive our sins and to cleanse us from all unrighteousness. If we say that we have never sinned, we are calling God a liar, and His word is not in us. My little children, I write these things to you so that you would not sin. But if anyone sins, we have an advocate with the Father, Jesus Christ the righteous.

That's God's promise of forgiveness. The three-in-one God (Father, Son, and Holy Spirit) does not look at our departures from what is right as something which isolates us forever from his love and presence. He does not demand our holiness or righteousness as a condition of our acceptance by him. He knows that we can never, in ourselves, measure up to his holiness and righteousness.

Thus, he has made a way for us to be forgiven of wrong and to be made right with him. His love reaches to us where we are, even standing in the gray areas. His love reaches to us when we are in the dark areas. And his love lifts us to a place of light. Jesus spoke words of comfort: "For God did not send His Son into the world to condemn the world, but that the world through Him might be saved" (John 3:17 MEV). And even to the woman taken in adultery, Jesus said, "Neither do I condemn you. Go, and sin no more" (John 8:11 MEV). For believers, here is the pledge of our Father God: "I, even I, am he that blotteth out thy transgressions for mine own sake, and will not remember thy sins" (Isa. 43:25). He shines light into our lives and forgives our sins, as the guarantor of our salvation.

As we saw earlier, Jesus is that light, and he told us to be light; furthermore, the apostles confirmed that commission. But if we are to be light, we must know the difference between the true light and the culturally-accepted false light of the deceiver, Satan. We must know the difference between light and dark, right and wrong. Even King David had to learn this the hard way. He let his eyes lead him to lust after a married woman who was beautiful and alluring. David convinced himself that he had a right to have Bathsheba, the wife of one of his most faithful soldiers. But she became pregnant, so David devised a plan to trick her husband, Uriah, into thinking the baby was his own. But the plan failed, and David's adultery compounded into murder (2 Sam. 11:2-27). Adultery and murder from the man who is called a man after God's own heart, as we see in Acts 13:22.

Did David feel the darkness of his error, as though in a dark pit when, after all that, the baby that resulted from his sin fell sick? Hear what he says in Psalm 88:3-6:

> *For my soul is full of troubles,*
> *And my life draws near to the grave.*
> *I am counted with those who go down to the pit;*
> *I am like a man who has no strength,*
> *Adrift among the dead,*
> *Like the slain who lie in the grave,*
> *Whom you remember no more,*
> *And who are cut off from Your hand.*
> *You have laid me in the lowest pit,*
> *In darkness, in the depths.* (NKJV)

However, as we see in Psalm 51 and others, his despair turned to hope when he repented and returned to the LORD, his "light" and "salvation" (Ps. 27:1).

Discussion Questions

1. Discuss movies or TV shows you have seen recently that opened you up to accepting as "right" some behavior which you

previously believed to be wrong (such as stealing when in need, taking revenge when justice seems to have failed, having an affair, or committing other sexual sins).

2. What Bible verses can you find that address that behavior or attitude? What do these verses say about it? Be sure to look at them in context and in coherence with other Bible verses.

Personal Reflection

1. Have you ever found yourself lost in the shadows or darkness (like Chapter 1 depicts) because of feelings, attitudes, or actions that took you off course and away from the Light of the Word?

2. Think about how that came about. Did it happen suddenly or did it come gradually, as you moved into the deepening shadows? Did you feel far from the Lord?

3. Have you found peace for that situation? Remember, our Lord is faithful and is only a breath away. He longs for us to call out to Him in our despair, to surrender to His gentle rescue.

Verses to Consider

1. Read Psalm 27:1 and 119:105; John 1:1, 9 and 12:46.

   (a) What is the connection between the Word, the Lord, and light?

   (b) What other Scriptures do you find that refer to Jesus as the light?

2. Read 1 Peter 2:9 and Colossians 1:13.

   (a) What general darkness have we been called out of?

   (b) What specific darkness have you been called out of?

3. Read Acts 26:18 and Ephesians 5:8-10.

   (a) What is God's purpose in delivering us from darkness?

   (b) Would you say that God desires to bless us with light, rather than to limit or stifle us?

CHAPTER 3

†

Disappearing Light

BEFORE WE WERE MARRIED, my husband had a pet canary. The little bird would sing its head off when my husband returned from work, especially when he let it out of the cage to fly around the house. It loved the freedom. It would land on my husband's head or shoulder and sing and chatter with glee. But it always went back to the cage when it was hungry or tired.

But alas, one day while flying around the house, cheerfully singing and enjoying its freedom, the bird seized an opportune moment when the front door opened. He was outside faster than my husband could respond. And outside lay the neighbor's cat, a blanket of snow, and lots of traffic. Needless to say, the little bird was gone. He didn't come back. Nor was he ever found.

He had left the security of home and had wandered into dangerous territory. Outside the safety of appropriate boundaries, his freedom became his downfall.

It's strange how many lessons we can draw from this poignant incident. First, we could view the cage as the law, which constrains us for our own good. Secondly, the liberty to fly around the house represents the life of grace. We are free to fly around our Master's (our Father's) dwelling, still within his safe, secure, righteous, godly, and loving boundaries. We are not under the law, bound by the cage, but we are constrained by the wall of God's love to live "soberly, righteously, and godly in this present world" (Titus 2:12).

We expose ourselves to danger when we venture outside God's righteous standards, in either attitude or behavior. Our thinking can become confused, our emotions battered, our bodies harmed by elements of a sick society, and our spirits attacked by devilish ideas. Peer pressure and the desire to be liked, social pressure to conform to current standards of morality (or lack thereof), and the overwhelming pressure to be politically correct in all manner of speech, attitude, and response—these forces all combine to present real threats to godly living. Add to that the temptations that plague our flesh—sexual, substance, or success—and we face more than we can handle when we go it alone.

Godly standards exist to protect us. Both the law and the admonitions of the New Testament writers operate for our good. Our loving heavenly Father has placed these boundaries there because of His deep love for us, for even "while we were yet sinners, Christ died for us" (Rom. 5:8).

If you are younger than twenty-five, this canary analogy may seem strange to you. You grew up in a society whose cultural values are not only "tolerance" but also "celebration" of that which earlier societies recognized as harmful, counter-productive, or unnatural: abortion on demand, especially late-term abortion (aka partial-birth abortion); pregnancy out of wedlock; co-habitation before marriage; single parenthood in general, except in cases of widowhood; and homosexuality, which, like illegal drug use, often results in AIDS, and which was previously viewed as perverted, even by those whose outlook wasn't particularly biblical.

You may have been raised free of a "playpen," and may not even know what one is. When my children were small, I relied on it to keep them from crawling into danger when I was busy in the kitchen or laundry room. Later, I could train them to keep objects out of electrical sockets or to not touch the hot stove. My mother has told me of the serious burns I had on my hands from leaning on the open oven door *after* she had cautioned me not to touch it. She was right: it was hot. Some of us have to learn the hard way, right?

We can use those cute little gates to keep babies and toddlers from staircases or to keep pets out of the pet-free zones in our homes. But who of us would allow a toddler or young child to roam freely outdoors unattended by older siblings, a babysitter or nanny, or ourselves? We set boundaries for a reason. So why wouldn't our loving heavenly Father? Just as we watch over our children, he watches over his. This idea is shown in the following verses from Psalm 139:1-4, 7, 13, 23-24 (NKJV).

O Lord, you have searched me and known me.
You know my sitting down and my rising up;
You understand my thought afar off.
You comprehend my path and my lying down,
And are acquainted with all my ways.
For there is not a word on my tongue,
But behold, O Lord, You know it altogether.

Where can I go from Your Spirit?
Or where can I flee from Your presence?

For You formed my inward parts;
You covered me in my mother's womb.

Search me, O God, and know my heart;
Try me, and know my anxieties;
And see if there is any wicked way in me,
And lead me in the way everlasting.

Indeed, when we realize how well he knows and watches over us, staying within his boundaries becomes both pleasant and desirable.

In that context, we learn that some things our society calls "okay," and even supports and promotes, are things which we should avoid. They are things which are contrary to the righteous word, will, and way of our Holy God. However, prevailing social pressure or temptation might bombard us and carry us into actions, behaviors, or attitudes that have crossed the lines of righteousness. This can happen so subtly that we may feel "okay" about it. We then find ourselves "outside the house."

Thus, we dare not rush toward the dangers that lie beyond the boundaries (as did my husband's pet canary), or willfully seek out the shadows that darken the pathways and steal our vision (as we saw in Chapter 1). To do so is self-destructive. It runs the risk of eroding relationships and destroying families, resulting in a ruined society.

The light disappears when we willfully break boundaries. But what happens when we just shift them, as when society begins to normalize behavior once thought to be wrong? Can we throw out all rules and make our own individual ones? After all, we live in a time when relativism prevails: what's true for one person is not counted as true for another, and so on, with multiple conflicting truths being all accepted as equally true. Here are a couple of illustrations:

(1) Once upon a time in a faraway land lived a group of people who had defeated all their foes and set up a kingdom of total liberty. The rulers of that country believed that rules and laws make people rebellious, so in order to avoid rebellion, they abolished all rules and laws. For a while, everyone was happy. But then the children became adults and carried their lack of discipline over into their adult lives. First, they robbed food from older citizens because it was easier than working. Then they traded their women back and forth, and the women grew to like that "variety," since everyone knows that "variety is the spice of life." It wasn't long, though, until jealousy set

in. One man killed another. Then another young person killed him, and so on. Pretty soon, no one was happy or safe. The rulers, having relinquished laws and rules, were ignored by the common people. No one was in control, and everyone did what he or she thought was right. Chaos soon destroyed the society.

(2) Near to that town was another group of people who had grown tired of the laws under which they had lived for many years. More and more, people were desiring to do things that had been prohibited—like sell or swap their spouses when they became bored or unhappy, or execute or sell their children when they couldn't train them, or kill off the older people rather than caring for them. It started gradually, of course, with no one really doing it outright. First, people watched those behaviors on TV and at the movies as fiction or make-believe. Then the celebrities began doing it, subtly at first, and no one seemed to complain. The media hailed it as revolutionary and hip. Pretty soon, others followed, the professional athletes first, then the politicians. Before long those new behaviors became the "new law" because they were considered to be the "new normal" and the "new morality." However, with so many people being sold, swapped, and killed, the population declined and people stopped working. After all, why work if you can be sold the next day and lose it all? Of course, once that happened, the economy crashed and famine set in. Chaos engulfed the society, and soon this town vanished, as had the first.

Those examples highlight two related problems: First, the removal of all moral laws; and second, the mutation of morality into what was formerly considered immoral. The removal of all moral laws is anarchy; the substitution of immoral for moral is rebellion. The Bible shows both of these conditions existing at different times in Israel's history. They are present in the Church also. Let's view these in action.

Removal of Moral Law

During the time of the judges in Israel's history, it is written twice that, "In those days there was no king in Israel: everyone did that which was right in his own eyes" (Judg. 17:6; 21:25 MEV). The first part of that verse is also found in Judges 18:1 and 19:1, revealing that the key was the lack of a godly ruler. Of course, God himself wanted to be their king, but they rejected him. The second part of that verse is found in Deuteronomy 12:8, after the giving of the law and the injunction to not follow the behavior of the godless people of the land: "You are not to do all the things that we are doing here today, where every man does whatever is right in his own eyes" (MEV).

In the New Testament, the apostle Paul instructs us that we are not under the law, but grace (Rom. 6:14). However, grace is not permission to sin. Grace teaches us to deny "ungodliness and worldly lusts" and to "live soberly, righteously, and godly, in this present world" (Titus 2:12). Our liberty under grace is to love one another, and so fulfill the law (Rom. 13:10). This is quite different from the first illustration of a city with no rules (and, consequently, no love), a city where people satisfy their own lusts, doing whatever is right in their own eyes.

Mutation of Moral Law

This mutation of morality is shown in the history of Israel by the way in which the kings ruled the land, promoting a watered-down version of the sacrifices and incorporating idol worship into the religious observances. King Ahaz even redesigned the altar of sacrifice and moved the God-ordained altar to the side. And the priest Urijah went along with these changes (2 Kings 16:10-15).

Ezekiel tells of the idolatry that was present even in the temple (Ezek. 8) and how the princes of Israel had led the people into all sorts of sins (Ezek. 22). These include idolatry, adultery, incest, murder for hire, exorbitant interest rates, extortion, theft, graft, and profaning the Sabbath day. The priests (like some modern-day clergy in some denominations) "put no difference between the holy and profane" (Ezek. 22:26).

In the New Testament, we see words spoken against the church in Thyatira, which represents the worldly church of all denominations (Rev. 2:20). By this point, the church had allowed unscriptural teachers who taught the people that adultery, pre-marital sex and other sexual sins, and worship of modern idols, among other things, were really okay. Of course, all this was done while doing good works on the surface—in the power of self, rather than of the Spirit: self-works, not works of true righteousness. This illustrates that second story, where the things which were called moral were really things which God has defined as immoral. Does this sound like today, where even Christian denominations preach acceptance of homosexuality and abortion?

Presence of Moral Law

In contrast, God sets the boundaries for our good. Jeremiah speaks of God's purpose for Israel, which is also applicable to believers in general: "For I know the plans I have for you, says the LORD, plans for peace and not for evil, to give you a future and a hope" (Jer. 29:11 MEV). Knowing this, we can rest in his boundaries and not desire the forbidden territory of disappearing light.

It becomes preferable to follow the admonition of Proverbs 3:5-6: "Trust in the LORD with all your heart, and lean not on your own understanding; in all your ways acknowledge Him, and He will direct your paths" (MEV). It becomes beneficial to follow the advice of Paul in Romans 12:2: "Do not be conformed to this world, but be transformed by the renewing of your mind, that you may prove what is the good and acceptable and perfect will of God" (MEV).

These verses show the need to not look to self or to others for one's standards of right and wrong, but to look to the Lord. They emphasize the goodness of God and the "rightness" of his will. The Old Testament is full of verses that show the blessings that come from doing life God's way. The contrast of righteousness with wickedness is as clear as light and darkness. Here are a couple of Scriptures to ponder while thinking about how our society is trying to change the nature of morality:

> Jehovah brings the counsel of the nations to nothing; He frustrates the plans of the peoples. Jehovah's counsel stands forever, the thoughts of His heart to all generations. Blessed is the nation whose God is Jehovah, the people He has chosen for His inheritance. (Ps. 33:10-12, Green, *The Interlinear Bible*, Vol. II)

> When the righteous rule, the people rejoice; but when the wicked rule, the people mourn. Where there is no revelation or vision, the people are let loose to perish; but happy is he who keeps the law. (Prov. 29:2, 18 author paraphrase)

Bringing this back to the case of my husband's canary, it's easy to see that when the canary chose to discard or replace his boundaries (the walls of the house), he flew to his death in the winter air where dangers lurked outside. Had he been content to dwell within my husband's house, he could have lived a longer, fuller, and happier life.

That little canary represents us. We need to stay within the boundaries of our heavenly Father's love and will. When we do, we will thrive and be blessed. The light will not disappear.

For us, although the dangers might not be as immediate as they were to the canary, they are real. We have a spiritual enemy waiting to pounce on us; we face the life-stealing power of spiritual coldness; and distractions of all sorts are primed to run us over, especially in the darkness.

Discussion Questions

1. Come up with a list of "do's" or "don'ts" that work for your protection and well-being. These should be stated like New Testament instructions rather than commandments, which we cannot keep in our own strength.

2. Realizing that we are not under the law, but under grace, think of New Testament admonitions for each of the Ten Commandments. Discuss these verses in terms of your experience of them as safeguards for you, with respect to your opinions, emotions, and actions.

3. Read Galatians 5:13-14 and 1 Peter 2:15-16. Do you see that being "not under the law" does not mean being "lawless"? Would you say that the law helps us to know what loving one another looks like? Discuss this idea.

4. List the contemporary issues or social pressures that push the boundaries of these instructions or commandments. Does political correctness mean that we must break God's instructions? Do we have to cross God's lines of righteousness in order to meet with society's approval?

5. This chapter uses Israel's idolatry as an example of breaking boundaries. Of course, idol worship is not really done in our country today. Or is it? Discuss what kinds of things serve as idols, taking our time, energy, and money. (I highly recommend Kyle Idleman's book *Gods at War: defeating the idols that battle*

for your heart. Grand Rapids: Zondervan, 2018. His book will open your eyes to potential idols in your life.)

6. Though we have a three-pronged governmental system, what else is needed to maintain public safety, social order, and individual responsibility in any nation? Is that being eroded in this country? Discuss what we, as Christians, can do in and for our society to help get us back on track. Is there any hope for the USA?

Personal Reflection

1. Given the lists produced in the discussion questions above, which instruction or boundary are you most likely to cross? Why?

2. Look for Bible verses for and against the behavior in question. Knowing that God never contradicts himself or his Word, can you reconcile your actions or attitudes with the Bible verses you found?

3. Would it be easier for you to live in a "birdcage" (the law) or in the "house" (grace)? Why? If you find the open world (free of godly restrictions) more preferable, why? Be honest with yourself and with God.

4. What biblical moral code do you feel is outdated, if any? Think about why you feel that it doesn't apply today. Look for verses that support your view. You can use a Strong's *Concordance*, or other reference book, or use www.blueletterbible.com and select various versions of the Bible, whereas Strong's is limited to the *King James Version*.

5. Now, objectively look for verses that support the biblical moral code. Why has God set up that moral code? Do you think it is just to be controlling? Or does he have our best in mind, like a parent who rightly tells the child that he cannot have candy before dinner?

Verses to Consider

1. Read Psalm 40:5 and 139:17-18; Jeremiah 29:11; and John 10:10.

    (a) Summarize the nature of God's thoughts toward us (you, specifically).

    (b) What do you think "abundant life" looks like? How would you describe it?

2. Read John 10:14-16 and 27-30. Think about Jesus' example of the sheepfold as a safe place where sheep are contained and protected from predators and thieves. Consider his example of the two divine hands that hold his people.

    (a) Consider which seems more secure and stable: (i) You must work to keep saved; or (ii) You are eternally secure in Christ.

    (b) Do you see that you are safe in the sheepfold? Would you like to be?

    (c) Do you see that you are safe in his hand and the Father's hand, and that you cannot be plucked out, unsaved, or stolen from God?

CHAPTER 4

†

Dark Origins

ON JULY 22, 1995 Susan Smith was convicted of killing her two young sons, having shocked the nation when she confessed that she had not been car-jacked as she originally claimed. Instead, she had intentionally killed her sons, a three-year-old and a fourteen-month-old. She had strapped them into their car seats and driven to a lake, climbed out, "put the car in drive, released the brake," and let the car roll forward from a boat ramp into the water. She had watched the car drift out and slowly sink with her children alive and sleeping. When she finally told officers the place where the car went down, they found it and retrieved the boys, "the small hand of one . . . pressed against a window." An autopsy proved they drowned.[1]

A Brown University study of FBI data shows that an average of 500 children are killed by their parents each year, and that almost 72% of victims were under seven years old. One-third of those were babies under one year old. In the deaths of the majority of those under seven years old, parents used "personal weapons" (fists and feet) to "beat, choke, or drown" their children.[2] Since 1995, there has been increasingly less focus in the news at each occurrence of child killing by a parent.

Besides untreated mental illness, what leads a parent to kill his or her own child?

We can sympathize with Susan Smith regarding her troubled childhood (sexual abuse by a stepfather after her own father committed suicide). But on a larger scale we have to ask, "What force in our society makes the killing of one's children the go-to plan of action for those who are clearly disturbed or troubled?"

Is it because life has little value (if any) in a pro-abortion, evolution-embracing society where a preborn baby is considered just a blob of tissue and where it is assumed that all life came about by chance, with no difference between humans and other animal species?

What children are taught in public school directly influences their view of life. They are, for the most part, taught to scorn the idea of an all-wise Creator who lovingly designed all that we see in this world. They are taught that life is a product of time and chance and that humans have no special "soul" different from any other animal. Moreover, documentaries and books predominantly enforce these positions. Being indoctrinated with such, what are they to think about the value of life?

Add to that the current trend of video games, movies, and even children's cartoons. What are the children to think and what values are they to grow up to hold? Certainly not the value of every human being. Certainly not the worth of each individual. Certainly not the specialness of the human race to a creator God to whom we are each accountable. Witness to this are the rising toll of gang murders in inner cities, sex trafficking, outrageous abortion rates, and all-too-common suspicious deaths, such as the one in D.C. recently where a two-month-old baby was found floating in the river. Add to that influence the sale of unborn baby parts as though the growing human is just a mass of tissue to be bartered on the open market.

When naturalistic evolution was posited as a theory, the unbelievers of the culture were quick to seize it as an alternate explanation for creation. They looked for evidence to support the theory. Thus, all sorts of things became "evidence." This is because scientists who set out to prove their own theory as true, whether it is or not, will skew their findings in their favor. (It is human nature to do so.) If they know from the beginning what they want to find, they will find it, even if it doesn't exist. They end up testing the evidence (and using what can be manipulated to fit the theory) instead of testing the theory in light of the evidence.

Eventually, the theory became taught as fact, with Biblical Creation pushed aside, mocked, and rejected. However, the real stretch of the imagination is the wildly random big bang, with odds greater than those of winning a state lottery. This is compounded by the speculation that species of animals unsuited to an environment can live in that environment for hundreds of thousands of years until they gradually mutate and adapt to such environment. Clearly, naturalistic evolution has as its purpose, not the scientific explanation of life on earth, but rather to supplant a creator God in order to remove our necessary human accountability to such a creator God.

How different becomes the view of human dignity and worth when we accept the presence of an all-wise Creator to whom we are each accountable. The reality of the Triune God—Father, Son, and Holy Spirit—is inextricably woven into the fabric of our physical reality. To believe that God is Creator of the universe, the planet, and every life form, every rock formation, and every body of water hereon, is to understand that we are not only "wonderfully made," but we are accountable to him for our actions and attitudes. To deny that he created the world, space, and life is to remove accountability and open the floodgates of sin.

The difference is like that of children in a loving home versus children abandoned on the streets. The former have parents to look after them and to supply their needs, parents who will train them up and hold them accountable for their actions. The latter will run wild, foraging for themselves. Without anyone to hold them accountable, they will likely enter a life of crime out of necessity for survival.

On a deeper level, the ones who believe in a creator God will find life precious and will most likely respect the worth of every individual, even unbelievers. Those who reject the Creator may consider life cheap and easily disposable when it doesn't fit their plans. I'm not saying that all who believe in naturalistic evolution hold life cheap, but that the natural outworking of that belief is to hold life cheap because there is no one to whom we are held accountable. We become our own attorney, judge, and jury. And who will readily admit fault or blame? Even Susan Smith fooled the country for over a week before she finally broke down and confessed.

Some would ask why an intelligent person could believe in God as Creator. For a discussion from a scientific standpoint, there are many books that answer this and refute naturalistic evolution. A partial list is provided in the endnotes.[3] This book takes the view that God created the heavens and the earth by the power of the Word, his Son, in the presence of the Holy Spirit. In John 1:1-5 and 9-10 we see this fact, which is also clear from Genesis 1.

In John's gospel, God reveals the existence of the Son from the beginning, and shows that the Son became a human being and dwelt on earth among people:

> In the beginning was the Word, and the Word was with God, and the Word was God. He was in the beginning with God. All things were created through Him, and without Him nothing was created that was created. In Him was life, and the life was the light of mankind. The light shines in darkness, but the darkness has not overcome it. (John 1:1-5 MEV)

Dark Origins

This was Christ, before he became the God-man Yeshua ha-Mashiach, Jesus the Messiah (Anointed One). And when Jesus came into the world, He came as "The true Light, which enlightens everyone . . . He was in the world, and the world was created through Him, yet the world did not know Him" (John 1:9-10 MEV). If they had known him, "they would not have crucified the Lord of glory" (1 Cor. 2:8).

In Genesis 1:1 we see the beginning of all earthly things as we know them: "In the beginning God created the heaven and the earth." We also see that something happened of which we have no knowledge now, but which altered the state of creation, because in verse 2 we read of a fallen earth: "And the earth was without form, and void; and darkness was upon the face of the deep. And the Spirit of God moved upon the face of the waters."

Did something happen between verses 1 and 2 to mar an original creation, a sort of sick-spell eons before the rest of the record here? Or did God start with a world in that condition of emptiness to make a point to us, an analogy of sorts? All we know for sure is that the earth, at that time, was dark, void, without form, and covered in water. We have no concept of what that dark and void earth looked like, what the elemental composition was, other than, if it was water, it was H_2O—hydrogen and oxygen atoms bonded together. But it was dark—totally dark in the absence of light.

This description of earth would speak of a previously formed planet which had been destroyed—marred by the darkness of spiritual evil. And into this darkness God spoke, "Let there be light. And there was light. And God saw the light, that it was good: and God divided the light from the darkness. And God called the light Day, and the darkness he called Night" (Gen. 1:3-5). This light came forth from the Son of God, who is the Light of the world (John 8:12; 9:5).

Notice that this division came about before the sun, moon, and stars were created. Light was called Day, and darkness was called

Night. Note the difference in terms. Day and Night represented the light and the darkness, but "evening and morning" constituted a period of time called a "day." Genesis 1:5 says, "And the evening and the morning were the first day." God used the terms evening and morning before there was even a sun to rise and set—or for the earth to revolve around. That is why the Apostle Paul could call believers "children of the day" rather than children "of the night" (1 Thess. 5:5). Here and in other places in the Bible, "Day" signifies the condition of spiritual light, while "Night" represents the condition of spiritual darkness.

It wasn't until the fourth day that God created the sun, moon, and stars. He even created the plant kingdom before these celestial bodies. He created sun, moon, and stars for several purposes:

> to divide the day [lower case, as different from Day in verse 5] from the night [also lower case]; and let them be for signs, and for seasons, and for days, and years: And let them be for lights in the firmament of the heaven to give light upon the earth: and it was so. (Gen. 1:14-15)

These were different from spiritual Day and Night. These were for physical tracking of time and for physical light for the benefit of creation. Verses 17 and 18 say, "And God set them in the firmament of the heaven to give light upon the earth, And to rule over the day and over the night, and to divide the light from the darkness." Again, this is speaking of physical light and darkness, not the spiritual Light and darkness of earlier verses.

Time could be measured and tracked by these lights—time, which is not needed in the spiritual realm but is a necessity in the physical realm. Even on a cloudy night, the moon and stars, though hidden, are still there, beyond the atmosphere. In most areas of the earth, the sun provides warmth even after night falls, even in Antarctica, which is really, really cold.

All species of fish and birds first, then mammals, reptiles, and amphibians were created after the sun, moon, and stars. Last of all to be created were humans, starting with one man, Adam. This might be one point that naturalistic evolution gets right—humans were the last species formed. However, their view that humans descended from earlier primates is way off course. God took special pains with people. Let's look at ten facts.

1. The Triune God (Father, Son, and Holy Spirit) planned the human race and agreed to share likeness with humans—giving them a soul, emotions, conscience, sentient property of reason, ability to choose to worship and obey God or not: in essence, free will. See Genesis 1:26-27.

2. God had a plan and a purpose for humans, which was to rule over and care for all creation. See Genesis 1:26.

3. God's image provided for both male and female—different genders or sexes, with no hint of a provision for their choice in the matter. See Genesis 1:27.

4. He gave them an immediate task. See Genesis 1:28.

5. He gave them a long-range provision. See Genesis 1:28.

6. He provided food for them. They were vegetarian at first, as was all the animal kingdom, which fed upon the vegetable kingdom, since death had not yet entered. See Genesis 1:29-30.

7. Adam was formed from the dust of the ground. See Genesis 2:7.

8. God breathed into his nostrils the breath of life—that free-will, soul/spirit breath that makes humans different from other mammals. See Genesis 2:7. Only of humans is it written that "man became a living soul." Proof that Adam had free will is shown in Genesis 2:16-17. Proof that Adam had the capacity to think and reason is found in the fact that he named all other life forms. See Genesis 2:19-20.

9. Woman was made from man. Adam did not cross over to become a woman. He did not make do with an animal. God made a woman from Adam and gave her to him as a separate being, a suitable companion, for the immediate purpose of fellowship and procreation. See Genesis 2:21-22. God's long-range purpose for woman was that she be a symbol for the spiritual union between God and those who love Him. See Ephesians 5:22-32.

10. There was no shame between the man and the woman. See Genesis 2:25. Shame entered after sin entered. Some people say that Christianity causes guilt. No. Sin causes guilt. Christianity provides release from the guilt by the forgiveness of God through faith in Jesus Christ, the Son of God, and acceptance of Him as Savior.

We will discuss this more fully in later chapters. For now, we see a five-fold importance of understanding the reality of a creator God and the presence of light as a source of life (John 1:4).

1. To recognize that spiritual light and spiritual darkness are real forces at work in our lives.

2. To understand that the Son of God is the true source of spiritual light and that he is greater than the forces of spiritual darkness.

3. To realize that he seeks to bless us with light, life, joy, peace, love, hope, forgiveness, reconciliation—"all spiritual blessings in heavenly places in Christ" (Eph. 1:3). Meanwhile, the forces of darkness seek to destroy, to bring the earth back under the dominion of darkness that existed before creation of the world as we see it in Genesis 1:2.

4. To know that ultimately the forces of darkness will lose, though they put up a good fight, as obvious today and in times past, and as will be more so in the future.

5. To be assured that light will win—the light that shone in Genesis 1:3 before the creation of sun, moon, and stars. God will be the source of light in heaven. See Revelation 21:23.

Therefore, it is important to see naturalistic evolution as the lie it is, even though it is now taught as fact in schools and in media under the manipulation of the forces of darkness. In a blog, "DNA Molecules and the Odds Against Evolution," Alan McDougall quotes two well-known scientists, Fred Hoyle and N. Chandra Wickramasinghe, in his article about the improbability of naturalistic evolution:

> The trouble is that there are about two thousand enzymes, and the chance of obtaining them all in a random trial is only one part in 10 to the 40,000power, an outrageously small probability that could not be faced even if the whole universe consisted of organic soup.[4]

He stresses that "10 to the 40,000power is a 1 with 40,000 zeros after it!"[5] Indeed, naturalistic evolution is so improbable as to be beyond belief, but if it were true, then the following ideas naturally follow:

1. Humans are only animals with nothing to look forward to but death.

2. There is no objective morality. Thus, pedophilia, rape, murder, and all other crimes are acceptable behavior.

3. There is no "higher power" or moral lawgiver to whom we are held accountable.

4. We might as well be dead, because there is no ultimate purpose centered outside ourselves.

Humans, under this lie, would eventually destroy the planet and bring back that darkness—apart from the intervention of a creator God.

This is the pit into which our fictional person from Chapter 1 has descended. And apart from the intervention of a loving God, our person will remain there in that darkness.

Discussion Questions

1. Discuss your view of creation vs. naturalistic evolution. Do you think that removing a creator also removes our accountability to God?

2. Consider the "evidence" presented for a big-bang and naturalistic evolution. Do you find those odds concerning? Does it seem possible that without an intelligent designer, the different species could arise on their own? Is it more likely that the supposed links between species, as seen in some fossils, were simply other species that became extinct over time?

3. Spend some time looking at the websites, https://www.allabout thejourney.org (particularly /spontaneous-generation.htm and /evidence-for-intelligent-design.htm) and https://www.allabout science.org/darwin-day.htm. These are websites by a 501(c)(3) corporation called AllAboutGod.com. They take a long view at the errors of Darwin's theory and the stubbornness of atheistic scientists who continue to force it to fit, regardless of the evidence to the contrary. They quote a scientist, George Wald, who, in 1954 published an article wherein he declares,

> When it comes to the origin of life there are only two possibilities: creation or spontaneous generation. There is no third way. Spontaneous generation was disproved one hundred years ago, but that leads us to only one other conclusion, that of supernatural creation. We cannot accept that on philosophical grounds; therefore, we choose to believe the impossible: that life arose spontaneously by chance![6]

Do you see that those who continue to believe naturalistic evolution in the face of all the evidence from microbiology, fossils, and mathematical probabilities, do so because they do not want to accept a creator to whom they are held accountable?

4. I.L. Cohen, a mathematician, researcher, author, and member of the New York Academy of Sciences, states in his book *Darwin was Wrong – A Study in Probabilities*, that

> every single concept advanced by the theory of evolution (and amended thereafter) is imaginary and it is not supported by the scientifically established facts of microbiology, fossils, and mathematical probability concepts. Darwin was wrong.[7]

Cohen also states that "The theory of evolution may be the worst mistake made in science."[8] (It is reported that Darwin himself regretted positing his theory, on his death bed.) Whether it was a deliberate lie designed to discount the Creator or a mistake made without evil intent, do you see the overall harm caused by the theory of evolution?

Personal Reflection

1. Do you want to have a creator God to whom you are accountable? Why or why not?

2. If there is no creator God, what is the purpose of life?

3. Can you find meaning in your life outside of yourself if there is no creator to whom you are accountable?

4. If people are the same as other animal species, what is the value of life? And is there an eternity to look forward to? Something beyond this life?

Verses to Consider

1. Read Psalm 33:6-9; Acts 14:15-17; Colossians 1:16-17; and Hebrews 1:2; 11:3.

    (a) Do you see that Jesus the Son is also the agent of creation? Truly, he is both Creator and Redeemer.

    (b) Does that magnify him in your eyes?

    (c) Are you ready to sing the song of Revelation 4:11?

2. Read Psalm 19:1, and Romans 1:20-23.

(a) Do you see proof of God in the stars, life forms and processes, and even in the smallest bacteria cells?

(b) How could our bodies function as they do as merely a result of chance?

(c) How could the planets maintain orbit as a matter of chance?

3. Read Romans 1:24-32, and 2 Thessalonians 2:3-11.

    (a) Do you see what the denial of God as Creator leads to?

    (b) Do you see how the beginning of that lie which leads people astray is possibly naturalistic evolution—the belief that everything happened by chance, out of nothing, with no creator to design it and give it purpose?

CHAPTER 5

†

Day of Darkness

IN THE LAST CHAPTER, we referred back to the dark pit into which our hypothetical person from Chapter 1 has plummeted. We contrasted the Light of the Lord of Life with the darkness of the destroying deceiver. We showed that naturalistic evolution, first theorized in 1809 and published in 1859, helped to bring about the beginning of cultural darkness in this country. Even though the theory has been revised of necessity (because it lacked credibility), even the revision has been proven erroneous. However, the effects on society remain. They remain because the theory is still taught as fact in our public schools and because other ideas have entered the culture as a direct result of that theory.

It is like a row of dominoes set on end. When the first one is pushed over, they all fall in succession, each knocking the other down. When the Creator was removed from social conscience, the next thing to fall was the understanding of objective morality: the knowledge of biblically defined good and evil, right and wrong. Thus entered relative morality or situational ethics, claiming that a behavior is right or wrong depending on the circumstances and that an action is good or bad depending on the situation. Closely related to this lack of clarity, the next domino to fall was the sense of truth. Truth also became relative and could, therefore, vary from person to person, group to group. Moreover, this pluralism opened the floodgates for chaos.

With an origin based on chance rather than on a creator to whom we are accountable, relativism easily entered and destroyed the concept of objective morality and absolute Truth. After all, if we are here by chance, then who's to say what is good or bad and true or false?

As we saw in Chapter 2, the entertainment media led the way in situational ethics, making revenge killing and adultery acceptable, and now making gay relationships the norm, as T.V. program after T.V. program features gays and lesbians, even showing intimate moments. Definitely a channel changer for me.

Only builders and boomers can recall the early days of television (such as *I Love Lucy*), where bedroom scenes showed married couples fully covered in pajamas and sleeping in twin beds. Some will chuckle at that prospect now. However, with that innocence and wholesomeness gone, we are left with shocking displays of sexuality and sin.

With moral relativism and pluralistic truths, anything goes. Pluralism advocates that whatever a person believes is true for that person and that all truths are equally true. The accepted thought is that all roads lead to heaven, all behaviors are subjective and therefore acceptable, and anyone who denies that is either "racist," "sexist," "homophobic," or a "religious fanatic."

The thing about relative morality is that it must be taken to be relative, not absolute. But those who believe it hold it as absolute, even while claiming there are no absolutes. Those who support "pluralistic truths" must accept as equally true the opposite belief that only one belief structure is true. This creates a conundrum, for if every person's truth is true, and my truth says that not every person's truth is true, then it must be accepted as true that not all truths are true. Talk about mental chaos and social disruption.

Think about how morality has mutated. As circumstances change and public opinion alters, behaviors which were formerly unacceptable become acceptable and accepted. The clear lines of conduct blur to the one who rejects absolute (objective) morality. This is because all behavior becomes a matter of personal choice when there is no moral lawgiver. But those choices have consequences which affect more people than just the person or persons who make them.

Builders and boomers can remember a time when having a baby in high school without being married was not celebrated and applauded. Teens who "got caught" in such a way were encouraged either to put the baby up for adoption or "do the right thing" and marry the baby's father. It took the sexual revolution of the 60s and 70s to change social conventions.

In 2016, according to the Center for Disease Control, 39.8% of births were to unmarried women.[1] This rate is actually down from the peak of 2007-2008, but the abortion rate has increased, as well as the availability of birth control and the increase of homosexual relationships, which, of course, don't include procreation. Medicaid paid for 42.6% of those births in 2016, which shows a financial effect on society of this change in moral standards. Most of us understand that there is also a social effect, as children in single-parent homes have a disadvantage, though many overcome it. And abortion definitely affects another: it ends the preborn child's life and life choices.

This is the "normal" that Generation Xers and Millennials have grown up with. Many Christians in these groups regard pre-marital sex, unwed pregnancy, abortion, and homosexuality as acceptable (more on that later). After all, we're told to "love one another" and to "judge not lest you be judged." However, loving one another does not necessitate accepting wrong behavior as right. And it is not judging another when it is judging behavior, not the person. Let me rephrase that: We can love one another without accepting as valid their wrong choices. We can, and we should.

Moreover, we can judge our own behavior and that of others as violating God's righteous standard without judging (condemning) the person and, in fact, while loving the person and seeking for their release from darkness. After all, if I see someone's house on fire, I should alert that person and call 911, not walk on by and say nothing, so as not to offend them. But this truth (love the person, not the sin) has been supplanted by relativism, a worldview that ignores basic definitions and, in fact, redefines any term that supports objective moral law and absolute truth.

Connected with this spread of relative morality is the excess of pleasure, the emphasis upon immediate gratification of desires (sexual or otherwise). From movies to music, from books to celebrities, from pre-teen tantrums through high school protests, we are taught to fulfill our wants as quickly as possible. But in the rush to find pleasure, we lose meaning. Ravi Zacharias has often quoted G. K. Chesterton who said, "Meaninglessness comes not from being weary of pain, but from being weary of pleasure."

As a culture, we have become so hedonistic that nothing truly important has meaning or value. Postmodern thought feeds into this as it teaches that language itself has no meaning because every word is related to another word, and so on, none of which can have an absolute meaning but are only social constructs. Their meaning is only assigned by groups of people who think alike, and different groups can assign different meanings to the same words. This gives rise to great chaos because words do have meaning. Water heated to 212 degrees Fahrenheit (the boiling point) cannot rationally be said to be cold.

I love the example of Os Guiness's which I heard Ravi Zacharias use about a baseball umpire. Under realism (where objective moral law and absolute truth existed), the umpire could say, "I call it what it is." Under modernism (which includes relativism), he would say, "I call it like I see it." Under post-modernism (which denies meaning altogether), the umpire says, "It's nothing until I call it." This makes the postmodern individual his own god, even over an event and the perception of it. What a division this sets up, because the next person may see the same event differently. Thus, we have the current day split between political parties and division between many different groups. Conflict abounds in our society because we have drifted so far away from a mutually-accepted moral code and a moral lawgiver to whom we are accountable, creator God.

This erosion of meaning leading to an increase in conflict is demonstrated by the current polarization of political parties, complete with all the petty bickering, name-calling, blame-throwing, and red herrings that seem to abound. We have a media that emphasizes one political and moral philosophy over the other and a liberal court system willing to collaborate in their persecution of both individuals and businesses that won't comply with the new morality (which is really immorality).

Furthermore, media and politicians call the conservatives (who believe in objective morality) intolerant, hateful, and bigoted, while they themselves display intolerance, hatred, and bigotry. The words mean nothing because they are so loosely tossed around. On his radio broadcast, "Just Thinking," Ravi Zacharias exposed this tendency of our culture to "moralize on politics and politicize morality." He said that the chaos would continue and worsen "unless language returns to meaning and moral values return to absolutes."[2]

Thus, the dominoes have fallen. First went the belief in our divinely-arranged origin; next went the belief in our divinely-inspired moral standards and absolute truth; next went the belief in absolute meaning. This downward cascade is unstoppable, apart from intervention. Just like with dominoes, the last item falls, and the last to fall is the belief in a hereafter based on scriptural truth.

How is the belief in heaven and hell distorted in our culture? Ever watch *Ghost Whisperer*? What about other T.V. shows or movies, like the 1990 Patrick Swayze hit, *Ghost*, or the 1999 Bruce Willis hit, *Sixth Sense*? Many shows portray the soul as living on as a spirit being, visible to those who are gifted. The spirit being wanders around until he or she finishes a task or receives closure. These movies do not accurately show what moving "into the light" really is. They portray moving into the light as the reward for anyone who lived a *good* life or whose disembodied spirit does a *good* deed after death.

These movies redefine *good* and disregard the necessity of faith in Christ. They discount biblical teaching that the soul leaves the body at the moment of death, and if the person has accepted Jesus as Savior, the soul moves to heaven—immediately (2 Cor. 5:6, 8). If the person has rejected Christ, the soul goes to a place other than heaven, referred to as Hades, hell, Sheol, and the grave. There they await the final judgment, as John sees in the visions he was given for the book of Revelation. In Revelation 20, we see the white throne judgment of the rest of the dead, who "lived not again until the thousand years were finished" (Rev. 20:5). In verse 13 of that chapter, we read "and death and hell delivered up the dead which were in them." My Bible has a marginal note regarding the word "hell," stating that the Greek word is "Hades, or the grave." Thus, we can conclude that the spirits of the dead do not linger on earth looking for closure, as modern spiritualism would have us believe.

This distortion of destiny provided by the entertainment industry brings the ultimate darkness, though all of these other "dominoes" are important: origin, truth, meaning, and destiny. Removing them one by one deepens the shadows and increases the darkness—just like we saw in Chapter 1 with the growing darkness that seemed to suck the person down into its dark pit. And that's the darkness that is growing in our culture today, darkening even the day.

The apostle Paul warned us of this condition in his letter to the Colossians. He writes, "Beware lest anyone captivate you through philosophy and vain deceit, in the tradition of men and the elementary principles of the world, and not after Christ" (Col. 2:8 MEV). The ideas of relativism, pluralism, post-modernism, and spiritualism are all worldly philosophies and vain deceit. Their traditions are rooted in humanism, not in Christ or the Word of God. As such, they are "the trickery of men, by craftiness and deceitful scheming" (Eph. 4:14 MEV). Hebrews 13:9 warns us, "Do not be carried away with diverse and strange doctrines" (MEV). Such error erodes truth and lessens the light.

For those desiring to walk in truth and light, the test of doctrines and philosophies is this: Do they agree with the Word of God? Not with a single Scripture taken out of context and forced to mean something other than what it contextually means, but the whole of Scripture as to the overriding principle of God's sovereign grace and goodness. If an idea leads to darkness, it is not of God. If it brings true light to our spirit and life, it is of God.

> This then is the message which we have heard of him, and declare unto you, that God is light, and in him is no darkness at all. If we say that we have fellowship with him, and walk in darkness, we lie, and do not the truth: But if we walk in the light, as he is in the light, we have fellowship one with another, and the blood of Jesus Christ his Son cleanseth us from all sin. (1 John 1:5-7)

If we have fellowship with God, we are walking in the light.

Discussion Questions

1. What strange doctrines have you heard that attempt to answer the questions of origin, meaning, morality, and destiny? Do movies or books portray them as valid? How would you answer those strange doctrines?

2. Have you heard of *soul sleeping*—which posits that the soul, even of a believer, sleeps in the grave or urn and does not get to heaven until the resurrection? Can you find Scriptures that support that? Can you reconcile that view with Philippians 1:23 and 2 Corinthians 5:6, 8, both of which discuss the prospect of physically dying and immediately being in the presence of the Lord?

3. What arguments have you heard that support the "new morality" of co-habitation before marriage, extra-marital sex, homosexual lifestyle, and abortion? Do these make sense to you? Do they line up with the whole of Scripture?

Personal Reflection

1. Are you already walking (or do you want to walk) in the light?

2. Do you agree with any of the philosophies, other than biblical Christianity, which were discussed in this chapter? Why? In a very human way, some of them do seem appealing. We all want to believe that everyone will be in heaven (except the serial killer, perhaps). But we all know good/nice people who don't believe in Jesus, but whom we'd like to see in heaven. All the more reason to pray for them and for a chance to witness to them.

Verses to Consider

1. Read John 6:29, 40, 47; 14:6; Acts 4:12; 1 Timothy 2:5; Revelation 5:9; Ephesians 2:8-9; Titus 3:4-7; Acts 2:21; and John 20:31.

(a) Do you see that there is only one way to heaven—faith in Jesus Christ?

(b) Do good works, apart from faith in Jesus Christ, qualify a person for heaven?

2. Read 1 John 4:15; 5:11-12; Acts 10:43; Hebrews 9:27-28; and Galatians 3:22, 26.

    (a) Do you understand that we become children of God by faith in Jesus Christ and are forgiven of sin and bound for heaven?

    (b) Do you see that we can do no works to replace or enhance his sacrificial death for us?

3. When God's judgment came on Israel for their idolatry and rebellion, it came as a "day of darkness." Read Joel 2:2; Zephaniah 1:14-15; and Amos 5:18.

    (a) Is it possible that the cultural darkness in this country is itself the beginning of God's judgment on our land for the rebellion of the people? Or will his judgment come later as a result of the darkness which we as a society have allowed to creep in? Could both scenarios be true?

    (b) Even if our culture is dark, must we live in that darkness?

4. Read Judges 17:6; 21:25; Deuteronomy 12:8; and Ephesians 4:17-19.

    (a) Does Deuteronomy 12:8 prohibit relative morality and situational ethics?

(b) Israel fell into these attitudes and actions to their national downfall, as we see in Judges. Can we expect a similar result, nationally?

(c) Since the unbelieving world subscribes to relative morality and situational ethics (steps toward humanism), as Christians are we to agree with them or stand apart from them, rejecting their influence?

CHAPTER 6

†

Absence of Light

IN THE PREVIOUS CHAPTER, we saw the foundational pillars of origin, truth, meaning, and destiny being overshadowed by cultural darkness. Imagine, if you will, waking up on a dark night when no moonlight streams in through the curtains. The power is off. The usual tiny lights that enable you to see your way around no longer glow: the digital clock with its LED display, the display on the air purifier, the toothbrush charger, the night-light which comes on only when it's dark and goes off in the daylight hours. Pitch black. Or at least almost. You reach for your cell phone which has the flashlight app, and you're good to go, though you have to watch your step lest you stub your toe or trip and fall.

The darkest place I've ever been was in a silver mine near Ouray, Colorado. Deep in the mine, the guides turned off the lights. It was pitch dark. It was darkness you could feel. That absolute darkness sparked panic in me. Paralyzed, I didn't dare take a step for fear of moving the wrong way and being separated from the group. I clung to my husband's hand for dear life. In that dark mine, even night-vision goggles would not have profited, since they work by amplifying existing light, however small its source. No light equals no amplification.

In that darkness, the guide told several stories about the use of birds in the mine and the use of candles to check for the presence of oxygen or harmful gasses. Then he turned the lights back on. What a relief! (In retrospect, I'm glad I wasn't wearing night-vision goggles, because what a shock I would have had when he turned the lights back on.) But I came away from that experience thinking about how dreadful it would be to have to live in a darkness that thick, that void, that terrifying. How could I, or anyone, live in a total absence of light?

Our culture is rapidly becoming that dark as it seeks to extinguish all traditional lights—biblical creation and authority, objective morality, logical meaning, and purposeful end. Its newest attack, and I say *newest* though it's been overtly going on since the 1990s, is "tolerance." We've seen how traditional morality has been eroded and corrupted by redefining what is good or evil. I remember when the general terms on report cards describing conduct were changed. "Good" and "Bad," often referred to as "Satisfactory" and "Unsatisfactory," were changed to "Standard" and "Non-standard." This resulted in a lessening of the seriousness of unsatisfactory behavior. It was merely non-standard.

Now, when I substitute, even as a para-educator with a trained teacher in the room, I sometimes see the majority of students in a classroom behaving in ways that were "unsatisfactory" fifty years ago. I hear the excuse from educators that "kids are different today" and we "just have to accept that." So what was once "Unsatisfactory" is now "Standard."

The same has happened with words like "tolerance," which used to mean "putting up with" deviant behavior or ideas while still recognizing them as destructive or, at the very least, counter-productive. Now the redefined meaning of "tolerance" has been set up as a prevailing standard of political correctness, making what formerly was defined as abnormal or deviant behavior into what is enforceable as normal and good.

How did we get here? It started with slight redefinitions of the term "tolerance." By that, I mean that the actual definition of "tolerance" has been revised continuously since the early 1900s. I suppose we would expect this of any word, since "gay" used to mean "lively; bright; sportive; merry; showy" according to a 1908 dictionary.[1] The same dictionary defines "tolerance" as "The toleration of offensive persons or opinions."[2] It defines "toleration" as "1. Allowance of what is not approved. 2. Liberty given to a minority to hold and express their own political or religious opinions."[3] To some people, that seems to be a harsh definition. It clearly sets out that certain behaviors are offensive and not approved, and that such actions or opinions are held by a minority.

A later book defines "tolerance" as "1. willingness to bear with others, especially those whose views differ from one's own; 2. the act of putting up with, or permitting to go on without interference, something not wholly approved."[4] Here we begin to see the invasion of relative morality: that which is "not wholly approved" is defined as "views [that] differ from one's own." The implication is that they aren't necessarily wrong or offensive, but that they are simply different. However, even with this definition, there is the thought of putting up with the behavior or belief without necessarily accepting it as correct or right.

But that soon eroded. In keeping with the changing absolutes, by 1990 the American definition of tolerance changed to "readiness to allow others to believe or act as they judge best."[5] And by 1998, the word became "(a): sympathy or indulgence for beliefs or practices differing from or conflicting with one's own; (b): the act of allowing something."[6] So we have gone from "putting up with" to "having sympathy for and indulging others in" their views or practices, which conflict with our own.

A look at the current definition creates even more disparity. The *Oxford Dictionary Online* defines "tolerance" more like the 1931 version. The popular, American online dictionary, *Dictionary.com,* gives a different spin to the word:

> 1. A fair, objective, and permissive attitude toward those whose opinions, beliefs, practices, racial or ethnic origins, etc., differ from one's own; freedom from bigotry.
>
> 2. A fair, objective, and permissive attitude toward opinions, beliefs, and practices that differ from one's own.
>
> 3. Interest in and concern for ideas, opinions, practices, etc., foreign to one's own; a liberal, undogmatic viewpoint.[7]

Thus, "tolerance" includes being permissive of people and their ideas and behaviors; it mandates that not being permissive is "intolerant," "unfair," and "bigoted."

Clearly, there is no longer a distinction between what is appropriate or right (as to actions and practices) and what one should tolerate or allow of others. In order to appear fair and objective (i.e., politically correct), one must be permissive of, concerned with, and sympathetic to those practices to which he or she objects. Our society has added to that the requirement of accepting as correct the views and behaviors of others, in order to be deemed sufficiently "tolerant." Thus, discernment of right and wrong, good and evil, light and dark is no longer permitted. It has been replaced with permissiveness toward that which is harmful, celebration of that to which one objects, and acceptance of such behaviors as normal and appropriate. Then let us all allow our children to play in traffic, to be tolerant of their choices and prove ourselves not to be bigots.

I prefer the 1993 British definition where tolerance is defined as "the ability to be fair and understanding to people whose ways, opinions, etc., are different from one's own."[8] We do need to be fair and understanding of people whose beliefs and actions differ from what we know aligns with the Word of God. We do not, however, need to accept their different beliefs and actions as right, correct, true, or otherwise acceptable. There is a difference between tolerating people and tolerating behavior. For example, we do not tolerate rape or murder, though we may tolerate the perpetrator and even pray for his or her salvation.

The same would apply to other so-called lesser offences, such as adultery, same-sex activities, or abortion. We do not accept such as being right, though we love the people, sympathize with them, and seek to understand and help them. Unfortunately, our culture has inverted the order, so that the behavior is to be tolerated (accepted and celebrated) at the expense of the person's temporal and eternal well-being.

On the other hand, the so-called tolerant left has no tolerance for those on the political right. A whole list of phobias is ascribed to us if we take a firm stand for what is biblically right, naturally normal, and innately beneficial for individuals, families, and society. This hypocrisy shows itself plainly, though the PC media refuse to recognize it.

Christians who decline to participate in the legitimization of behavior which contradicts the Word of God find themselves facing lawsuits, steep fines, and even closure of their businesses, on top of public scorn by so-called journalists and self-willed celebrities. Politicians who attempt to do what is reasonable for national security find themselves shut down by PC judges, in addition to being harassed and misquoted by the PC media.

Everything is tolerated except that which is based on traditional, biblical authority. If we call good "good" and evil "evil," then we are deemed to be intolerant and in no way are tolerated by society. True Christian light is not tolerated, which leads to more confusion and darkness in an already dark and confused culture.

Let me say here that some things that political correctness claims the credit for are really things that objective morality dictates as correct, such as showing kindness to all. The banning of certain disparaging terms, with respect to race and IQ, is not really centered in political correctness. It is something which Christian love dictates. So, when I talk about politically correct tolerance, I'm not putting down those constraints, but rather exposing the promotion of sinful and harmful practices as normal and good.

Therefore, what is our answer? To succumb to the PC culture? Many have, as they use isolated Scriptures to support a distorted "love" that celebrates destructive lifestyles. They have dropped the last phrase from the old adage, "God loved me where I was, but He loved me enough to not let me stay there."

Yes, God loves the person who has had an abortion. He loves the person caught up in homosexuality or other sexual sins. He loves the person whose life is a mess as a result of substance abuse and addiction. But in his love, he desires to bring them out of those conditions, to forgive them, to give them a new and abundant life. And he expects us who have experienced his love to love them that same way, with a love that would see them transformed, enriched, and established in God and his Word.

Thus, PC tolerance is like putting out the light in the silver mine. It ushers in the acceptability of "wrong" and calls it "right." It switches "darkness" for "light," and vice versa. It justifies "the wicked for reward," and takes "away the righteousness of the righteous from him" (Isa. 5:23). On one hand, it celebrates sin and perversity. On the other, it privatizes faith and worship. It has taken the homosexual out of the closet and put the Christian into the closet.

So, do we just stand terrorized in the dark and cling to one another for comfort, as in the silver mine? Or do we use what light we have (figuratively, cell phone, flashlight, matchstick) to illuminate the darkness?

What did God do when "the earth was without form, and void" and "darkness was upon the face of the deep"? (Gen. 1:2). He spoke light into the darkness. And that is what we must do: speak the light we have into the dark culture we are in. This is our cure for PC tolerance: to speak the truth in love. In Ephesians 4:14-15, Paul explains the purpose and path to spiritual maturity. It is that

> we may no longer be children, tossed here and there by waves and carried about with every wind of doctrine by the trickery of men, by craftiness and with deceitful scheming. But, speaking the truth in love, we may grow up in all things into Him, who is the head, Christ Himself. (MEV)

In that way, we flip on the switch in the dark mine.

Discussion Questions

1. Discuss what "tolerance" means to you.

2. Do you see the subtlety of its redefinition over time? How has this impacted your life personally? How has it affected your family or church? Other groups you are associated with?

3. Discuss the "new morality" that you see around you, arising from "political correctness." Is it really "morality" in the sense of God's righteousness, or has there been a redefinition of that word also?

Personal Reflection

Think of life in the oceans' deepest part, the Challenger Deep in the Mariana Straight. You can read about it here, https://www.marianatrench.com/ and http://www.deepseachallenge.com/the-expedition/mariana-trench/. Nearly seven miles below the surface of the ocean, it is deep enough to bury Mt. Everest with over a mile to spare. The water pressure at the bottom is nearly eight tons per square inch, about a thousand times the atmospheric pressure at sea level. The water is nearly freezing, and you can imagine how dark it is down there, that far from the sunlight, since at five hundred feet deep (less than one-tenth of a mile), little or no sunlight is perceptible, and the human eye cannot see colors.

There are hydrothermal vents which release highly acidic water at temperatures around 570 degrees Fahrenheit. The hot water dissipates into the cold water of the ocean floor, keeping the life forms from boiling. Some of the animals at that depth have bioluminescent appendages and features, which aid in mating, self-preservation, and hunting. Bioluminescence is defined as the "giving off of light by certain organisms."[9] That light is generated by an internal chemical reaction. The only surface animal that has bioluminescence is the Firefly, aka, Lightning Bug. Thus, in that darkness, creatures created by God are able to give off light enough for necessary functions.

1. With that in mind, do you see that God can enable you to be light in this dark culture?

2. Do you feel adequately equipped to be that light?

3. I mentioned that Christians have been put into the closet. Does that apply in your life? Have you privatized your faith to the point of hiding your candle under your bed? (See Luke 8:16.) Or do people know that you are a committed Christian?

Verses to Consider

1. Read Psalm 36:9; 43:3; 119:105; and Proverbs 4:18-19.

Absence of Light

- (a) Do you see that God's luminescence is what gives us light and enables us to see?

- (b) Do you believe that his Word will light your way?

- (c) Do you agree that you can be a shining light to others, lighting their pathway as God lights yours?

- (d) Do you see the importance of studying God's Word, so that you will know what his light is?

2. Read 1 John 1:5-7 and James 1:17.

    - (a) Do you see your responsibility to walk in God's light and to be light to others?

    - (b) Do you see that in God there is no shadow, no gray area that we can leave up to society to decide the morality of? Do you think that is "intolerant" of God? Does it intimidate you?

    - (c) Is it clear to you that some things that are politically correct are not, in reality, biblically correct?

CHAPTER 7

†

Works of Darkness

ANYONE WHO HAS EVER played pin the tail on the donkey or pin the diaper on the baby knows how difficult it is to hit the mark while blindfolded. I can still recall very clearly my experience at a baby shower for my dual-ethnic grandson. First, let me make clear that I don't like shower games. I am not a game player. I tried very hard to not participate. However, when my turn came, there was no getting out of it.

Second, let's just say upfront that I have worn glasses since the early primary grades. I am accustomed to functioning with partial sight. I have even observed how those who are blind function. One learns to compensate. To set a cup down, one feels with one hand for the coaster, table, or whatever, and then puts down the cup with the other hand in that spot.

So, here I am, blindfolded and spun around and around, brought to a stop in front of the large poster to which I was to pin a cutout diaper onto a baby. Having looked at it before my turn, I had unintentionally memorized the level of the baby and how far from each edge that baby was on the large poster. So, I reached out with my hands, got my bearings, and pinned the diaper perfectly where it needed to be.

I heard someone whisper to another, "She cheated." Needless to say, I didn't think of it as cheating. It was just a game, after all. I thought that was the object—to actually complete the task, win the baby gift, and give the gift to the mother-to-be. My first reaction was in my defense: If they hadn't wanted me to pin the diaper on the baby, they should have pointed me in a different direction instead of right in front of the poster. Then I would have stumbled blindly around, trying to feel my way and not being able to connect with the poster board.

In hindsight, I realize that, culturally, I should have "failed" so that someone else—one of the children perhaps—could have won, because the game stopped with me and no one else took a try at it. I had wanted to fit in but had done the very thing that set me apart from that daughter-in-law's family and friends.

Being blindfolded, though, can leave a person off balance. One might really think she's going the right direction, but discover she is way off course once the blindfold is removed.

Did you ever wake up at night and feel your way through your dark house? Even though you know the house—where the furniture is, how many steps (approximately) down the hallway—you still run your hands along the walls and feel for objects to keep from stubbing your toe or banging into something. Gradually, though, your eyes become adjusted to the dark, and you can actually see where you are going, especially if a little light glows from the plugged in electric toothbrush, cell phone, or GFCI socket, or if the moonlight filters in through a gap in the curtains.

Sometimes our life is like that. We may follow an impulse, discover that we feel lost or alone, stumble around until we get our bearings, and then begin to see dimly. We may mistake that shadowy and faint light for true light and convince ourselves that we are walking in light, that our actions are okay. After all, we didn't trip and fall down.

Yet.

Sometimes those situations are the hardest to classify as to rightness or wrongness. What we are doing may feel so right and yet be completely wrong, as with King David and Bathsheba, as we saw in Chapter 2.

I have had a friendship which I convinced myself was God-ordained and completely spiritual. In fact, I believed I had heard the Spirit urging me forward in that relationship. But the friendship I had with that other man began to erode my marriage. When I realized that I was spending more time and energy trying to spiritually encourage someone else's husband than I was in validating and appreciating my own, I tried to end the friendship—or at least the amount of time spent on it in phone calls. But the friend would not let go.

It was like I had drifted along in the shadows for so long, nurturing that relationship, that when I realized I was really in darkness, I was trapped. I had to acknowledge that the friendship was wrong, though everything on T.V. and in the movies would say, "Oh, no, it's okay."

Moral relativism would tell me that I had a right to my own friends, whoever they be. Political correctness would tell me that my husband didn't have the right to—as P.C. puts it—"control me like that." But I knew in my heart and spirit that the Word of God says otherwise. I had no peace or sense of light until I agreed with the Word and asked the Lord to end the relationship. Then I had a slow climb back to the full light of the truth of the Word of God and the repair of my marriage. Now I make it a point to limit my discussions with other men to either writing projects or scriptural topics. The Apostle Paul said it best: "I determined not to know anything among you, save [except] Jesus Christ, and him crucified" (1 Cor. 2:2).

And this is the condition that political correctness has brought us to—that state of confusion and chaos where we aren't sure what is right or wrong, what is good or evil, what is light or dark. In fact, our children are being taught to be confused about their own body's sex/gender.

Girls who used to be called "tomboys" and allowed to figure it out when they hit puberty are now directed to think of themselves as boys, use the boys' restroom, dress as boys, and be addressed with masculine pronouns. They are given hormones to block their system from entering female puberty.

Boys who are somewhat effeminate are directed to think of themselves as girls, use the girls' restroom, dress as girls, and be addressed with feminine pronouns. They are given hormones to block their system from entering male puberty.

Giving high-powered medicine (or any medicine) when none is needed used to be called child abuse. But politically correct new absolutes have changed that. With no concept of goodness, truth, and beauty, how can our youth be expected to know when life begins, what sex they are, or what sex they ought to be attracted to?

As a substitute teacher, I have found it difficult to call a middle schooler whose name is Andrea by the name of Andrew, and though she looks like a girl, to remember to use the pronouns "he, him, and his" in connection with her. Errrrr, him . . . whatever. (Of course, I changed the names here to protect the innocent.)

Additionally, I recoil from the thought that I might have to listen as children read from a new children's novel, *There's a Boy in the Girl's Bathroom,* which is geared to indoctrinate while teaching literature and grammar for grade levels 4-8. I believe that I would look for alternate literature on such occasion. Unfortunately, regular teachers might not have such opportunity, since they are mandated to meet certain guidelines and teach specified topics.

On a positive note, though, when I was substituting as a para for eighth graders, one student saw that title in the library and read it aloud. Then he added his analysis: "Ewww. That's just wrong." So, there is hope that not all children have been corrupted beyond help. Parents and grandparents need to take an active role in guiding their children and grandchildren.

As I write, the Christian Film and Television Commission has informed me of two new cartoon series geared for preschoolers. Both of these feature transvestite superheroes, cross-dressed characters designed to *normalize* this behavior to our children and grandchildren.[1]

Also, according to Family Policy Alliance, in at least forty states the public libraries have agreed to schedule (or have already held) Drag Queen Story Hours, where cross-dressing readers in horrid make-up engage with children in an effort to *normalize* their deviance.[2] The drag queens read books that promote LGBT ideology to kids as young as preschool.[3] I have to admit I am shocked that our society has arrived at this place, but, at the same time, I know how it happened.

This is nothing new, for "there is no new thing under the sun" (Eccl. 1:9). The apostle Paul discusses this downward spiral of humans in his letter to the Romans. It's an oft-repeated pattern which only seems to reverse in times of massive revival and return to God. Then, as shown in Psalm 107, the decline is repeated. Read Romans 1:21-32 in whatever version Bible you have. I prefer the KJV, NKJV, or MEV, but I will quote it here from *The Interlinear Greek-English New Testament*, supplying explanatory synonyms in square brackets, to use today's diction. You should notice the similarity to your version of choice. This portion follows Paul's discussion that the created world gives sufficient witness of God's existence, and his assertion that people who reject God are, therefore, without excuse.

Victory through Light

Because knowing God, they did not glorify Him as God, nor were thankful; but became vain in their reasonings, and their undiscerning heart was darkened. Professing to be wise, they became foolish, and changed the glory of the incorruptible God into a likeness of an image of corruptible man, and of birds, and four-footed animals, and creeping things. Because of this, God gave them up to uncleanness in the lusts of their hearts, their bodies to be dishonored among themselves; who changed the truth of God into the lie, and worshipped and served the created thing more than the Creator, who is blessed forever. Amen.

Because of this, God gave them up to dishonorable passions, for even their females changed the natural use to that contrary to nature [lesbianism]. And likewise, the males also forsaking the natural use of the female burned in their lust toward one another, males with males working out s h a m e f u l n e s s, and receiving back in themselves the penalty fitting their error.

And even as they did not think fit to acknowledge God, God gave them up to a reprobate mind [backwards, illogical, unable to think critically, a mind absent of judgment, unable to discern good or evil], to do the things not right, having been filled with all unrighteousness, fornication, iniquity, covetousness, malice; being full of envy, murder, quarrels, deceit, evil habits; becoming whisperers, slanderers, God-haters, insolent, proud, braggarts, devisers of evil things, disobedient to parents, without discernment, perfidious [unfaithful and disloyal], without natural affection, unforgiving, unmerciful—who knowing the righteous order of God, that those practicing such things are worthy of death, not only do them, but also heartily approve of and applaud those practicing them. (Rom. 1:21-32)[4]

In these verses, we see God giving humans up in their bodies (vv. 24-25), hearts (vv. 26-27), and minds (v. 28), which unleashed the long list of negative charges against humanity.

Some would say, "Well, then, it's God's fault because he gave up on us." But note that he didn't give humanity over until they left him. And even today, human departure from God is physical, emotional, and mental.

In the day Paul wrote this, the Romans and Greeks believed that an elaborate system of gods, goddesses, and demi-gods created and controlled the natural world. They worshipped idols fashioned like various animals or created things. In our culture, naturalistic evolution replaced creation, removing the creator God from the picture. In both societies, the people professed to be wise but were really foolish.

They continued to banish God from every area of life. They rejected truth, goodness, and beauty (which God desires to fill our lives with) and chose lies, perversion, and shamefulness. They chose darkness instead of light, just as Jesus spoke of in John 3:19-21:

> And this is the condemnation, that the light has come into the world, and men loved darkness rather than light, because their deeds were evil. For everyone practicing evil hates the light and does not come to the light, lest his deeds should be exposed. But he who does the truth comes to the light, that his deeds may be clearly seen, that they have been done in God. (NKJV)

And that is the darkness of our culture today, with what seems to be only a few choosing the light.

That's why I'm thrilled when I watch live videos of evangelists like Pastor Greg Laurie speaking the Word to crowds of thousands and when hundreds, and even thousands, respond to the call to be saved. Such a response from hungry hearts gives me hope that our culture has not become so dark it is beyond rescue.

But there is a tipping point, let's call it "critical mass," which, once arrived at, there will be no possibility of reversing the direction. Though "critical mass" basically means the "smallest amount of material needed to sustain a chain reaction, nuclear or otherwise," I often think of the term when I change the water in my backyard birdbath. There comes that point at which critical mass is achieved—the bowl is full and the reaction of water running over the edge is unstoppable. Every time I fill that birdbath, I think of our culture and how close we are to that point of no return in our downward spiral into wickedness.

That's why it's so urgent for us to stand for godliness and pray for those who don't yet know the Lord Jesus. We should pray for all those who now validate the ones caught up in the reprobate mindset of our society. We must believe that, at least for individuals if not for society as a whole, there is yet hope of repentance, reversal, and reconciliation.

An interesting thing to note here is that, quite often, the person who fits the description of Romans 1:28-32 is quick to point to Romans 2:1, and accuse the godly of hypocrisy: "Therefore you are without excuse, O man, whoever you are who judges, for when you judge another, you condemn yourself, for you who judge do the same things" (MEV). We may be quick to conclude that we aren't supposed to judge whether anyone is doing right or wrong, because calling sin "sin" is as bad as sinning. That's how many people take that verse, twisting its true meaning.

However, we must keep in mind that when Paul wrote this letter, he didn't put in chapter breaks. This thought is a continuation of the preceding chapter. It follows the verse that talks about people who consent to these wrong behaviors and even applaud the doers. The "judgment" refers to judging sinful practices as okay. When we accept as "good" any sin in others, we become a doer of that sin ourselves. The key for us is to love the person but hate the sin.

If we see a person in a condition of sin, love constrains us to warn that person. If we say nothing, we are like the citizens in Hans Christian Anderson's fairy tale, "The Emperor's New Clothes," afraid to tell the Emperor that his new clothes were non-existent and he was naked. After all, civility prompts us to alert others to danger, especially if they are unaware of it. Furthermore, if we hear someone calling for help, should we not help, even if just to call 911 for police to intervene? How much more do we need to respond to something of eternal significance?

A vital key is "speaking the truth in love," as we have seen in an earlier chapter. To the person who is truly confused by our culture and blinded to what is right or wrong, a harsh word of correction does little good. Our sincere love for them, as individuals with inherent value to God and to us, must be clear to them. We can share our own testimonies and experiences coming out of darkness and sin. Beyond that, the best thing we can do is point the person to the Word of God and let the Holy Spirit minister to them to bring about repentance and reconciliation. And, of course, we need to pray they will choose the light.

Some of the most confusing questions for our time concern issues surrounding our gender or sex, our sexual identity, sexual preferences, and the beginning of life—conception or birth. I refused to allow students to write papers about these delicate issues when I taught at the university level. The topics are too emotion-stirring, and our feelings can influence our thoughts and hinder critical thinking. As a wise acquaintance of mine once said, "I never met a feeling I could trust."

I believe that the Word of God, not feelings, should govern our view on these topics. Whenever I find myself questioning God about matters pertaining to righteousness, I am reminded of the counsel of a dear friend and church elder: "What does the Word say?" As Psalm 43:3 says, "O send out thy light and thy truth: let them lead me." Therefore, let's look at what the Word says about these sensitive topics.

First, let's look at when life begins—a critical part of the abortion argument. It's disconcerting to see the statistics about how many Christians accept abortion as okay. According to the Guttmacher

Institute, quoted on *Abort73.com*, "In 2014, 30% of aborting women identified themselves as Protestant and 24% identified themselves as Catholic."[5] Thus, over half of abortions (54%) in 2014 were by women who professed faith in Jesus Christ.

To these women I would say, "I understand. I get the whole 'it's just tissue' argument. It can seem logical." After all, in those early stages, the embryo and, later, the fetus, cannot live on its own outside the womb. But any woman who has felt the movement of life inside her knows that, tissue or not, a live little person grows inside. However, when the pregnancy is not planned, and, in fact, complicates life, when it results from a non-monogamous relationship or a non-consensual act, it's easier to think of it as "just tissue" rather than a living being.

But when post-abortion remorse hits, I also know that God loves us and is ready and able to forgive. I can say that because of my experience before *Roe v. Wade*. Having had an abortion before that decision (not law), I understand the working of the mind that chooses that option. I also know the overwhelming guilt that usually follows at some point. It did for me. I am thankful that I had, by that time, returned to the Lord. After I'd yielded my life to him, I was able to repent of the abortion/murder of that tiny unborn child and to understand that his or her little soul had already gone to heaven. I don't say that flippantly. It is often the only consolation there is.

What excuse did I have? I was single, a college student, and scared. I was too selfish to change my lifestyle for even enough months to carry to term and then adopt out, as my doctor recommended. I didn't want my parents to know. But the Lord didn't let me get away with that.

Before *Roe v. Wade*, "back alley" abortions weren't always in an alley, but there were often many complications, as was my experience. Underage and hemorrhaging, I had to call my parents for permission for lifesaving surgery. So, they found out anyway. My mother had suffered prior miscarriages, and I didn't realize until much later the emotional effect my abortion had on her. (Incidentally, complications still exist in so-called safe clinics, many of which fail to pass medical health inspections.)

Can I sympathize with women who choose abortion? Yes. But I also understand the resultant guilt and remorse that can consume a person, leading to depression, loss of worth, or emotional numbness—because I've been there. God helped me through the guilt of my past. He reminded me of his forgiveness and grace that I had already received when I accepted Jesus as my Savior. He helped me see my aborted child as safe in his arms.

I don't know what form the aborted children will have when our bodies are glorified, but I do read that "we shall be like him; for we shall see him as he is" (1 John 3:2). Furthermore, I know that "absent from the body" is "to be present with the Lord," as Paul says in 2 Corinthians 5:8. When an aborted child dies, his or her soul is present with the Lord, and he or she will have a glorified body some day.

How can I be so sure? Because of what the Word says about the life of the person in the womb. Psalm 139:13 in the NKJV reads, "For You formed my inward parts; You covered me in my mother's womb." The MEV words it, "You brought my inner parts into being; You wove me in my mother's womb." God recognizes the preborn baby as an individual.

If that were the only reference to God's work in the womb, we might be able to explain it away. But again and again we see his handiwork over what the abortionist calls "fetal tissue." Samson was to be a Nazarite, devoted to God "from the womb" till his death (Judg. 13:5, 7). Also, David spoke of belonging to God even in the womb (Pss. 22:9-10 and 71:6), as he spoke prophetically of Christ and also regarding himself.

Additionally, Isaiah uses that terminology, often in connection with the nation of Israel, unified or split (Isa. 44:2, 24). Isaiah and Jeremiah also speak of themselves as being formed by God from the womb. See Isaiah 49:1, 5 and Jeremiah 1:5. Though Isaiah speaks prophetically of Christ and, to a limited extent, of himself, Jeremiah's words are those of God to him in his call to ministry: "Before I formed you in the womb I knew you; Before you were born I sanctified you; I ordained you a prophet to the nations" (NJKV). This verse truly shows that God knows us from the zygote to the tiny embryo, through all the stages of fetal development, until we are born. We are not "just tissue." We are individuals whom God knows and loves.

Moreover, we see examples where God knew babies in the womb and what was in store for them. Of Rebecca and Isaac's twins, God declared, "Two nations are in thy womb, and two manner of people . . . the one people shall be stronger than the other people; and the elder shall serve the younger" (Gen. 25:23).

It was written of John the Baptist that he would be "filled with the Holy Ghost, even from his mother's womb" (Luke 1:15). He was even able to hear the voice of Mary and to leap in response—not to her but to the younger baby in her womb, Jesus (Luke 1:41, 44).

And in Galatians 1:15, the apostle Paul affirms, "it pleased God, who set me apart since I was in my mother's womb and called me by his grace" (MEV).

These verses make it clear that life starts at conception. The individual is a person at that point, known by God. Agreeing with the Word in that one thing solves so much of the chaos around us. If life begins at conception, it is a real person in the womb. Therefore, the life in the womb is to be protected as precious and unique, known to God.

Furthermore, if God knows the individual from the womb and if he takes responsibility for forming it, he knows if that life is a boy or girl. He fashions it accordingly. He doesn't make mistakes. If the organs are male, the child is a boy; if the organs are female, the child is a girl. It's only when we reject the sovereignty of God and his Word that we find ourselves plagued with gender confusion and sexual identity chaos. We mix misguided feelings with fact, listen to deceitful whispers of reprobate minds, and thus distort and devalue the facts.

In Job's final speech, he declares that the same one who made him "in the womb" also made his manservant and maidservant (Job 31:15). Of course, that One was God. And note, "manservant and maidservant"—two specific genders, easily identifiable. The writer of Ecclesiastes, Solomon, wrote that even as we humans don't really know the way of the wind or how the "bones grow in the womb of her who is with child," we don't really know the whole "work of God, who has made everything" (Eccl. 11:5).

Yes, we can trace wind patterns and explain why it blows, but we can't control it or predict wind bursts or exact tornado and hurricane appearances and paths. Microbiologists can explain that the sperm and egg unite, and how cells divide, and so on, but we can't really grasp the concept of how that happens. We really can't explain the world around us.

And that's because God has made that world, even down to the baby in the womb, and we are not as smart as God. Furthermore, he has made the baby in the womb either male or female, boy or girl, not transgender. When we agree with his Word in this, confusion and darkness vanishes.

Discussion Questions

1. Discuss the issue of boys using girls' restrooms and showers, and vice versa. Think about how that plays in to the larger issue of transgenderism.

2. How does transgenderism fit with homosexuality? Is it a way to explain away same-sex attraction? But in making that excuse, isn't the transgendered person admitting that boys should be

attracted to girls and girls to boys? If a girl thinks she's a boy, would she be attracted to girls or boys? Do you see how the confusion multiplies into chaos once we disregard God's natural order?

3. If you have children or grandchildren, would you allow them to watch cartoon series such as *Drag Tots* and *Super Drags*? Why or why not? Would you allow them to attend a Drag Queen Story Hour at a public library? Why or why not? Discuss what you can do to offer moral, Christian story hours for young children.

4. Read and discuss the verses cited about when life begins. Do you see why removing God as Creator is so important to the nonbeliever? If there is no God, then society can set the time that the unborn become persons. And if society sets the time, they are free to abort, even up to the left-leaning proposal of thirty-six weeks.

Personal Reflection

1. Have you or someone you know had an abortion? Do you realize that whatever attitude you have about it, God loves you? Do you know that he has covered that deed with the blood of his Son, Jesus, so that you can be free to live a full life in him?

2. Do you or someone you know identify with the opposite gender, as though the brain is one sex and the organs another? Do you see that the confusion comes from not acknowledging God as Creator who makes no mistakes? Unnatural or wrong urges are a result of the condition of sin into which all humans are born. Being born-again places us in a realm—the new creation—

where we can overcome sin because Jesus overcame it for us. See 2 Corinthians 5:17, 21.

Verses to Consider

1. With Romans 1:21-32 in mind, read Galatians 5:19-21; 2 Timothy 3:1-5; Ephesians 5:3-4; and Colossians 3:5-9.

    (a) Do you see a common thread of what God calls sin? Sexual sins, including homosexuality are listed, among others.

    (b) There are several items that pertain to attitudes, such as "hatred" (hostility, opposition); "lasciviousness" (lusting, filthy-minded); "emulations" (jealousies or indignation); "foolish talking" (silly talk or clowning about serious things); and "jesting" (vulgar joking or debased wit). Is "being confused" in that list? (You won't find it there.) Being confused is a condition that comes as a result of living in our culture without the light of God's Word to guide us. And there is no communication or bond between light and darkness, as 2 Corinthians 6:14 makes clear.

    (c) "Being confused" about gender or preferences is not a sin. It's a condition that springs from lack of faith in God and insufficient knowledge of his Word. And that can be remedied by calling on his name and asking him for wisdom. See James 1:5-8.

2. Read Acts 20:29-32.

    (a) Do you see the importance of the Word in our growth and decision-making?

(b) Do you notice that Paul said "word of his grace," not "word of his law"?

3. Read 2 Corinthians 4:3-6; Romans 1:16-17; 1 Corinthians 1:18; 1 Peter 2:21-25; and Colossians 1:12-14.

   (a) With 2 Corinthians 4:6 in mind, has the "light of the knowledge of the glory of God in the face of Jesus Christ" shined on you? If not, would you like it to?

   (b) Have you experienced redemption and forgiveness of sins? If not, would you like to? Do you see how those blessings are connected to the Light which Jesus is?

CHAPTER 8

†

Artificial Lights

WHAT DO WE DO IF we're in the dark and we see an artificial light, an unreliable light from an unknown source, a light that blurs reality and causes us to misstep?

Let's return to our hypothetical person in the dark pit, from Chapter 1, now that we understand how we got there. Our society deceived us; our culture misled us; and now we know that something must change. Where did we end? Oh, yes . . . like this:

The darkness settles upon you like a mist, and you know you are in the land of darkness, the black shadow of death around you. Will this last forever? You pinch yourself. You feel it. No dream. Is this what dying feels like? Are you even alive?

You hear moaning and wheezing around you and smell the stench of mold and rotting meat. "Give me light," you plead.

You find yourself hyperventilating, sucking in the horrid smells around you. Your lungs feel as though they are filling with liquid darkness. You scream, but only air comes out.

Victory through Light

"Give me a light," you whisper. Suddenly a pulsating strobe light shatters the darkness with its short, super-bright flashes that distort movement and call into question your eyesight, your sanity. It's like a rock concert without the music. Your movements appear jerky and slow, arrested sporadically. It seems like all action is frozen in the darkness. Dizziness overtakes you, but there is no rail to lean on.

It is a light. It's what you asked for, though not really what you had in mind when you called for a light. You were hoping for a steady beam of light you could see by, not this rapidly-flashing, sickening light that distorts your every move.

You look down at your feet. A gaudy neon light flashes from below you in the pit, sending out bursts of blue, pink, lavender, chartreuse, and yellow. The only words you can make out are "self-righteous works" and "hate."

That light isn't what you wanted either. It's not light to show the way. Besides, it beckons you down deeper into the pit.

You hear the hum of a machine and look around. The walls of the pit glow dark purple, like blue denim jeans under certain lights at night. It is black light, which uses ultraviolet light that can't be seen by the human eye. Only its effect on certain substances is visible. That's how you know it's there. And it feels like it's pulling you into it, though you resist.

Strobe light above, neon lights below, and black light around. None of them do you any good. In fact, their flashing glow and weird effects make you sick. You feel hypnotized and paralyzed. The blinding darkness seemed better than this. You open your mouth to scream. The word "Stop" echoes back to you from all sides, pulsating like the strobe light. Is there no escape?

Let's step away for a moment and discuss the three kinds of light that appeared to you in the pit. They are obviously artificial lights. But what do they represent?

Strobe Lights—Distorting Reality

Strobe lights are artificial, rapidly-flashing, high-intensity lights that play tricks on us. They symbolize vain philosophies of new age and "new Christianity." These are so-called new ideas that deny the truth of the Word, twist the Word, or simply ignore the Word to create a belief structure apart from sound doctrine. These are the philosophies of humans designed to spoil, condemn, and defraud those who fall into their trap.

The apostle Paul discusses them in part in Colossians 2:8, 16, and 18. We've already seen some of them, such as naturalistic evolution, relative morality, post-modernism, and politically correct tolerance. And there are more. Though it's impossible to list all of them here, a partial list includes ideas like these:

a) A good God wouldn't want anyone to go to hell, so everyone gets a ticket to heaven no matter what—or some variation of that with a few exceptions, such as for Hitler, Pol Pot, etc. (I've heard it as a question more than once: How could a good God condemn people to hell?)

b) All beliefs lead to heaven because everyone is basically good at heart, so it doesn't matter what you believe, as long as you are sincere.

c) All other religions worship the same God. They just call him by different names.

d) God made people as they are, so he loves them as they are and accepts their choices as good, as long as they are loving one another (i.e., homosexuality is okay with God). He doesn't try to change anyone.

e) Doctrine separates, so there's no need for it. We just all need to get along.

f) Jesus was a good man, a prophet, but didn't really die or rise from the dead.

g) There is no hereafter: you just live on in the memories of the people who love you. So, you make your own heaven or hell on earth.

Each of these misstatements (lies) can be countered with the truth of God's Word. Though they might sound "nice" to the human ear, they are deceptive and can only lead to greater darkness. For example, if the first three are true, then Jesus didn't have to be crucified and God made a mistake in planning that from the foundation of the world. See Revelation 13:8 and 1 Peter 1:18-21, which follow, with italics added by author:

> And all that dwell upon the earth shall worship him [the anti-Christ or beast], whose names are not written in the book of life of the Lamb slain *from the foundation of the world*.

> [Y]e were not redeemed with corruptible things, as silver and gold . . . But with the precious blood of Christ, as of a lamb without blemish and without spot: Who verily was foreordained *before the foundation of the world*, but was manifest in these last times for you, Who by him do believe in God, that raised him up from the dead, and gave him glory; that your faith and hope might be in God.

If the erroneous statements (a) through (g), above, are true, Christ died in vain, and not only in vain, but needlessly. Since God doesn't make mistakes, those erroneous statements cannot be true. Specific verses to counter each point follow, though there are many more for each point:

a) It's true that God doesn't want people to go to hell, but he provided only one way of escape. We really only need that one way. See 2 Peter 3:9, 10; Romans 2:4-9; 2 Peter 2:1, 4-10; and Ezekiel 18:23.

b) If all ways lead to heaven, then Jesus died needlessly and God himself spoke untruth. See Isaiah 42:8; 44:6; 45:5, 18, 22; 1 Timothy 2:5; Acts 4:10-12; John 3:16-21; 10:9-13; and 14:6. Besides, people are NOT basically good at heart. See Jeremiah 17:9; Psalm 14:1; Romans 3:10, 11, 23; 5:8, 12; and Galatians 3:22.

c) Acts 4:10-12 states clearly that there is no name by which we can be saved other than the name of Jesus Christ. He is one with the Father and Holy Spirit—three persons, one God, the Trinity. This triune God is also known as Jehovah (Yahweh), Elohim (plural in Hebrew); Adonai; the LORD; the I AM; the Holy One of Israel. See also Isaiah 42:8; 45:5; Deuteronomy 4:35; and Philippians 2:9-11. All other religions worship false gods, and all false gods ultimately are of the devil. We must understand that when God said, "Let us make man in our image," in Genesis. 1:26, he demonstrated the plurality of the Godhead. This is seen also at the baptism of Jesus on earth when the Father spoke from heaven regarding the Son who was on earth, and the Holy Spirit, like a dove, rested upon the Son, as seen in Matthew 3:16-17; Mark 1:10-11; Luke 3:21-22; and John 1:32-34.

d) Belief in Christ and his death for us brings new life to us, a life that is righteous with the righteousness of God. See Romans 6:4, 11-13, 18, and 22; 1 Corinthians 6:9-11; 2 Corinthians 5:17, 21; and Titus 2:11-13. Yes, "God so loved the world," but his work is a new creation, changing us from sin into his righteousness.

e) Doctrine is the gospel of truth. We are to stand for it. People who claim we must be open-minded have missed the point: they need to have open hearts. See 2 Timothy 1:13; 4:3-4; Titus 1:9, 14; 2:1; 2 John 4, 7-8; Jude vv. 3-4; Hebrews 4:14; 10:23; 2 Thessalonians 3:6; Romans 16:17; Ephesians 5:6-13; and 2 John v. 10. True, we try to get along with all, but we are not to closely fellowship with those who reject the truth and scorn our Lord and Savior Jesus Christ. Also see 1 Timothy 1:4 and 4:1-2, 7.

f) There is sufficient testimony that Jesus did rise from the dead. Had the Pharisees been able to produce his body, they could have easily squelched the movement of faith. See Mark 15:44-45; 16:6, 9; Luke 24:23; John 19:33-34; 20:1-18; Acts 1:1-4; 3:26. Read the many gospel records of Jesus' appearances to the disciples and others after his resurrection, last of all to Saul/Paul on the road to Damascus in Acts 9:3-6.

g) If living on in people's memories is all there is, then when all the people who remember us die, we cease to be. And though our life choices can make us feel like we're in heaven or hell (happy or miserable), there are real places described in the Bible where we will experience our afterlife. See Luke 16:19-31; 23:43; John 14:1-4; 2 Corinthians 5:1, 8; 12:2-4; and Revelation, chapters 1, 4, 5, 7, 14, 19, 20, 21, and 22, to name a few.

Like a strobe light, false ideas pulsate and appear to arrest motion. One cannot advance in the presence of such artificial light. Error cannot pull us out of the dark pit. But what of the neon lights encountered in the pit?

The neon lights flash pastel colors below you. Though the colors are pleasant, the incessant speed of their flashing irritates and nauseates you.

Neon Lights—Advertising Unprofitable Goods

Neon lights are colorful ionized gasses glowing in electrified glass tubes. These artificial neon lights represent ideas and people that foster hate and intolerance, self-righteousness and self-works. These are the factions or sects that practice hatred of homosexuals to the point of screaming denouncement of them (not the deeds, but the individuals).

The name of one such group springs easily to my mind because they also crashed funerals of military men killed in action in the Mideast: Fred Phelps's followers of Westboro Baptist, denounced by both the Southern Baptist Convention and Baptist World Alliance, as well as by many Primitive Baptist congregations. There was nothing Christian about their hate-filled, confrontational, discord-sowing behavior. In fact, they resemble radical Muslims who throw gays off rooftops and justify killing those who don't live by their laws or who shame their family.

Neither of those extremes provide a way out of the dark. Hating people who break a self-works code of behavior does no more than invite greater separation from the true Light, Jesus Christ. Darkness increases where there is no love. "Love one another," we are told (John 13:34 and 15:12, 17), for "God is love" (1 John 4:16).

To preach hate, to live hate, and to spread hate runs counter to all that Christ desires for us. It beckons us into greater darkness. Unfortunately, it has become politically correct for a certain political party that rejects God in its platform to spread hate, incite others to hate, and then accuse the other party, and Christians, of hating.

Another neon light is legality. Legalists insist that Christ's death was not enough to save us or keep us saved and claim that we must add our own works to his sacrifice. This error is like flashy neon lights, signage that leads into darkness as surely as the neon flashing of the Las Vegas strip or inner city skid rows.

When we hold ourselves to a self-works code of behavior, we increase the darkness around us. This is because there is no work we can do to finish what Jesus already finished. He declared salvation "finished" at the cross (John 19:30), and his resurrection sealed our justification by faith (Rom. 3:28; 4:16, 22-25).

This neon light of legality and self-righteousness flashes like a treacherous illusion. Dr. Veith says that legality is the

> true barrier to Jesus Christ. All rejection of God's grace takes this form. Those who refuse the free forgiveness of God through Christ do so because they do not see themselves as needing that forgiveness. They do not admit that they are sinners. They deny that they are desperately lost.[1]

This false light tells you that you are not even in a precarious position, that the situation of darkness around you is normal, non-threatening, and positive. It seeks to keep you from looking for a way out of the darkness, a way to be rescued.

We have covered this before, but it bears repeating. Our salvation is by faith in Jesus Christ, because of who he is and what he did for us. Paul writes in Ephesians 2:8-9, "For by grace are ye saved through faith; and that not of yourselves: it is the gift of God: Not of works, lest any man should boast." In this he makes clear that we can do no work to get saved or keep saved. In his letter to Titus, he writes, "Not by works of righteousness which we have done, but according to his mercy he saved us" (Titus 3:5), thus pointing to God's mercy and grace that saves us as we believe in him.

Jesus himself stated the need for faith—and only faith: "For God so loved the world that he gave his only begotten son that whosoever believeth in him should not perish but have everlasting life" (John 3:16). It is of prime importance to know of a certainty that we can do NO work to be saved. To presume that we could or must is to insult God. Jesus himself said, "This is the work of God, that ye believe on him whom he hath sent" (John 6:29).

So what is the point of the law, if we aren't expected to keep it? It was given to show our need of a Savior. Paul says in Romans 3:20 that "by the law is the knowledge of sin." He expounds upon this idea in Romans 7:7 and Galatians 3:8-14, 23-26, and concludes in 1 Timothy 1:9-10 that the law was made

> for the lawless and disobedient, for the ungodly and for sinners, for unholy and profane, for murderers of fathers and murderers of mothers, for manslayers, For whoremongers, for them that defile themselves with mankind, for menstealers, for liars, for perjured persons, and if there be any other thing that is contrary to sound doctrine.

The law is to govern the actions of those who reject God and his righteousness.

These are the very people of whom Jesus speaks in Luke 16:31, regarding unbelievers: "If they hear not Moses and the prophets, neither will they be persuaded, though one rose from the dead." Those who ignore the law as a standard of righteousness, who reject the reality of the creator God, who refuse to listen to the promise of a Savior and a way back to God—these will never see the truth of the light and grace of our Lord Jesus Christ. Those who reject Moses reject the creation which he recorded under divine inspiration, and they reject the law as God gave it to Israel through Moses. If they reject the law and the lawgiver, they also deny sin, and, denying sin, they are lawless.

Since they are lawless, they see no need for prophecies of a Savior, of one who forgives sin and gives new life. In fact, they hate those who love that truth and who attempt to enlighten them with it. See Matthew 24:10-12. Verse 10 speaks directly to our culture today: "And then shall many be offended, and shall betray one another, and shall hate one another." Isn't political correctness quick to claim, "I'm offended by that cross, nativity scene, and expression 'Merry Christmas'"? And from the offence come lawsuits, ridicule, vandalism, and hatred.

Another neon light flashing in the darkness is that of politically correct tolerance, which, as we saw in an earlier chapter, is simply the acceptance and celebration of sin. Current tolerance seeks to normalize deviant behavior. It is not a slippery slope fallacy to say that once homosexuality is fully accepted, pedophilia and bestiality will be next. There is already a push to accept an adult's sexual "love" of a child as a normal expression of love. The fact is that a certain non-Christian religion practices pedophilia, as did its founder in the 7th century.

This tolerance has infected the American military while partnered with foreign forces where pedophilia is the norm. The online magazine *Townhall* reports about an incident and ruling in a September 23, 2015, article by Katie Pavlich that tells about several injustices. After eleven years of outstanding service, Charles Martland was discharged from the Army for roughing up the Afghan military commander who bragged about chaining a boy to his bed for seven days and raping him repeatedly, as well as beating the boy's mother when she tried to protect her son. American soldiers were instructed to ignore the cries of these young boys being sexually abused by Afghan military because "it's their culture."[2]

This "look-the-other-way" attitude had prevailed in the military in Afghanistan since 2012 and before, according to an article in the *New York Times*. That online article tells about Special Forces Captain Dan Quinn, who was relieved of command after he fought with an Afghan militia leader who had chained a boy to his bed as a sex slave.[3] This occurred in 2012. Many others reported that abuse in 2012 and before.

Instead of receiving commendation or medals, these soldiers were punished for calling attention to the pedophilia and rape and for attempting to stop it. When the American military compromises morality in that way, we know that our culture is deteriorating. When we tolerate wrongdoing in others because it's part of their culture, our own culture suffers. When wrong is called right, when good is called evil, and when darkness is called light, then woe and deep darkness will cover the land.

Artificial Lights

But back to our hypothetical person in the dark pit. Neither strobe light above nor neon lights below are able to lift one out of the darkness. But then there's that black light:

A third artificial light begins to glow all around you. A deep purple glow. Indigo. It reminds you of the way your skin looks when the doctor checks it with an ultraviolet light. But this one seems to pull at you. It's like a magnet drawing you toward it, toward all the sides. Its force makes you feel like you will be torn apart, as it pulls you in all directions. How will you escape?

Black Light—Exposing Flaws, Faults, and Failures

This one symbolizes idolatry and the forces of darkness. Materialism, with its love of and desire for possessions, sets up idols for us to worship. These can be tangible, like houses, cars, jewels, a large bank account, and so on, or intangible, like success and fame. These idols are as misleading as the forces of darkness which parade as light.

One such force of darkness is the Wicca religion, which presents itself as harmless. It claims to seek harmony with nature and use only so-called "white magic." It has sanitized its image and deceived a generation of biblically-illiterate young people looking for answers in everything but Christianity. However, its worship of Satan reveals its true nature—darkness and not light.

So how many Wicca followers (i.e., witches) are there? Shockingly, the Pew Research Center reported that in 2014, there were approximately 1 million to 1.5 million Americans who identified as Wicca or pagan—0.4% of the population of the United States.[4] That was over five years ago from this printing, so the number is probably larger now. Since Wicca and paganism are two are separate ideologies, even half that number as witches would be half to three-quarters of a million.

Statistics about Wicca are scarce. However, a 2018 report by the managing director of the Center for Studies on New Religions, in Turin, Italy, provides interesting estimates for the United States. He says there are some eighty covens and pagan groups in the New York City metropolitan area and that 734,000 Americans identify as Wiccan or pagan.[5]

Witchcraft has become culturally palatable and politically correct, partly through entertainment media and partly as a logical outworking of the new age movement. How many remember (or watch reruns) of the sitcom *Bewitched* (1964-1972), where witches were either good-looking or somewhat humorous, always powerful but harmless?

On the darker side, spiritualism (which includes the belief that the spirits of the dead can communicate with living people by way of a medium) misleads many and distorts the true nature of death, as we discussed in Chapter 5. In our pit, this error glows as infrared light, hiding itself and showing up only through its effects—false notions, dread, deception, distorted reality. This was a practice that was forbidden under the law, as we see in Deuteronomy 18:10-12.

This is the Old Testament wizardry and sorcery that God despises because those practices disturb and defile people. Leviticus 19:31 says, "Regard not them that have familiar spirits, neither seek after wizards, to be defiled by them: I am the LORD your God." Those who had familiar spirits were said to be able to call up the dead. And if we look at 1 Samuel 28:7-19, at least one time it proved to be so. This was when King Saul resorted to asking a woman who had a familiar spirit to call up the prophet Samuel for him.

Samuel's spirit arrived, but his news was not what Saul wanted to hear. Samuel confirmed that God would remove Saul as king and replace him with David—because of Saul's earlier disobedience, to which Samuel had pronounced, "For rebellion is as the sin of witchcraft, and stubbornness is as iniquity and idolatry. Because thou hast rejected the word of the LORD, he hath also rejected thee from being king" (1 Sam. 15:23).

Note that the Bible doesn't say that no one can conjure up the spirit of a dead person, but it says that to engage in that practice is deceptive and that it defiles people. It turns our world dark, because it dabbles in the realm of death. Television shows and movies may make light of séances and such, but those engender darkness and not light. There is a force that does specialize in the realm of death and defilement, Satan. We'll see more about that devil in the next chapter. Suffice it to say, for now, that the ultraviolet light will not lead us out of the pit either.

Tests of Light

But aside from their effect on us, how do we tell a false light from a true light? How do we know that these things represented by the strobe light, the neon lights, and the black light are wrong ideas, especially when our culture tells us daily that one or more of them are good, moral, and beneficial values for our society and for us as individuals?

When a politically correct society pushes diversity, relativity, and anarchy in the name of openness, tolerance, and compassion, what are we to do? When we see our national identity and God-given heritage slipping away and our personal rights being eroded, especially those of religious liberty and free speech, how are we to respond?

In the Old Testament, the instructions were clear. God warned Israel about false prophets and set up two tests of a prophet's veracity. First, if he spoke against the Word, he was false and not to be believed (Isa. 8:20). Second, if what he prophesied did not come to pass, he was false and not to be believed (Deut. 18:22).

Both of these tests were to be met, not just one, as is clear from Deuteronomy 13:1-3. There we see that if the sign or wonder came to pass but the prophet urged forsaking God for idolatry, then the people were to "not hearken unto the words of that prophet, or that dreamer of dreams." Why? Because "the LORD your God proveth you, to know whether ye love the LORD your God with all your heart and with all your soul."

Note that God doesn't send the false prophet to test his people, but if a false prophet comes, God will see from the reaction of his people just where their loyalty is.

Likewise, even today we are to test the spirits and prophets, the spirits being behind the ideas and values of the culture and the prophets being the preachers and teachers. John states this very clearly in 1 John 4:1-3.

> Beloved, do not believe every spirit, but test the spirits to see whether they are from God, because many false prophets have gone out into the world. This is how you know the Spirit of God: Every spirit that confesses that Jesus Christ has come in the flesh is from God, and every spirit that does not confess that Jesus Christ has come in the flesh is not from God. This is the spirit of the antichrist, which you have heard is coming and is already in the world. (MEV)

Jude says that these false spirits/prophets "have secretly crept in" and "are ungodly men, who pervert the grace of our God into immorality and deny the only Lord God and our Lord Jesus Christ" (Jude v. 4 MEV).

Those who "pervert the grace of God into immorality" are those who claim that God accepts homosexuality (and other sex-related sins) as normal and good, because he is a loving God. True, he is a loving God, and he does love homosexual people. However, he desires to deliver them from that sinful condition and practice, one which rebels against his created order.

Those who "deny the only Lord God and our Lord Jesus Christ" are those who claim that Jesus' sacrifice on Calvary was not enough and they must work to be saved, or that other religions worship the same God but by a different name. They may insist that all roads lead to heaven if we are kind at heart. They claim that Jesus didn't really die or wasn't really raised from the dead. They think that he was just a man, not divine. Any of those modern day lies (which actually date back to the first century A.D.) emanate from false spirits.

Paul's epistle to the Galatians is full of warnings against false teaching, particularly legality, which insists that Christ's work is not enough and we must add to it certain works. He says that legality is an attempt to "pervert the gospel of Christ," and states emphatically that those who "preach any other gospel unto you than that which we have preached unto you, let him be accursed" (Gal. 1:7-9).

For more about this, see all of Galatians 1; 2:16, 20-21; and 3:22, 26, where Paul emphasizes our salvation by faith in Christ's completed work. And Paul gives a solemn warning in Acts 20:29-30 against false teachers: "For I know this, that after my departing shall grievous wolves enter in among you, not sparing the flock. Also of your own selves shall men arise, speaking perverse things, to draw away disciples after them." Peter gives a similar warning in 2 Peter 2:1.

And so we come to the place where we are willing to admit that false spirits have even invaded the church and have all but destroyed our culture. They have brought us to a dark place; moreover, in that dark place with all its so-called tolerance, openness, and diversity of thought, our culture offers no sufficient light for our escape. Can it get any darker?

Discussion Questions

1. Have you experienced the actual types of light used as symbols, such as strobe light, nauseating neon lights, or an ultraviolet light? Did they play tricks on your vision?

2. Do you consider as true light any of the ideas that this chapter lists as artificial or false light? Can you find sufficient scriptural support that would say they are true light? Discuss those with others, keeping an open mind.

Personal Reflection

1. Do you see how the entertainment industry feeds the false spirits that promote error? List some movies or programs (or even songs) that encourage false light.

2. Do you know how to test the spirits? Have you had to do that in your life? What was the result?

Verses to Consider

1. Read 1 Timothy 6:3-5; 2 Timothy 3:1-7; 2 John vv. 9-11; Titus 1:10-11; and Romans 16:17.

    (a) How do false words reveal wrong attitudes and result in wrong deeds?

    (b) Spiritually speaking, how does artificial light symbolize the presence of false ideas?

(c) Do you see that we are not to fellowship with those who propose false ideas, who put good for evil and evil for good, light for dark and dark for light?

2. Read Romans 3:20, 23, 28; and 2 Corinthians 5:21.

    (a) Can someone earn his or her way to heaven by their own works?

    (b) Do you understand that God provided his Son as a sacrifice, to die in our place, taking our sin to the cross, and that God raised him from the dead so that we would have new life?

    (c) Is any message that contradicts this essential truth a message of error?

3. Read James 1:17; Psalm 27:1; and 2 Timothy 1:13.

    (a) Paul speaks of the "breastplate of faith and love" in 1 Thessalonians 5:8, where the Greek word translated "faith" means "truth, gospel, reliance upon Christ for salvation, and conviction," and the Greek word for love expresses the agape love that God has for us, that same love that is "shed abroad in our hearts by the Holy Spirit" (Rom. 5:5 MEV). Do you see that holding the truth, rejecting error, and loving God and others are all interwoven in our new life, like cords of a strong rope?

    (b) Do you understand that calling error "error" does not mean we are unloving? That calling sin "sin" does not make us hateful? Love for others should always be our motivation, even in trying the spirits.

CHAPTER 9

✝

The False Light

IN CHAPTER 8, WE ASKED the questions, "Can it get any darker?" and "How will you escape?" We left our hypothetical person standing on a small patch of firm ground surrounded by deep and total darkness amidst three kinds of artificial light. Let's continue from there:

As the strobe light pulses above, the neon lights flash below, and the ultraviolet light glows around you, a hissing voice speaks to you. It sounds like it's coming from all directions. "Step off that solid ground that keeps you from enjoying the darkness." Chills shoot outward from your spine to every cell. You recoil in horror.

Then all the false lights go out. A strange light floats up to you from the dark bottom of the pit. The hissing voice continues: "If you will follow me, I'll show you how to be your own god. I'll give you power, wealth, and fame—whatever you want—if you come to me. You will be free to be and do what you want, to chase your wildest dreams, to satisfy yourself with whatever pleasure you choose. Oh, I will show you the way. Just take that step, close your eyes, and give in to me." There is an eeriness to the voice and to the appearance of that light, but its hypnotic effect is hard to resist.

Is this the light you've been searching for? It seems so seductive and evasive. Its promises sound liberating, drawing you away from the small patch of solid ground, but they seem laced with deceit and delusion. The light seems now to surround you, though you still can't see anything else. Is it possible to see what seems like light and at the same time to be surrounded by darkness? You reach out to touch what is there. Zapped with a small electric shock, you draw your hand back and cross your arms in front of you in a defensive posture.

From outside the pit, a different and melodic voice calls: "Even Satan disguises himself as an angel of light" (2 Cor. 11:14 MEV). You squeeze your eyes together and extend your arm, an index finger pointing. "Go away," you say to the eerie light. Immediately it's extinguished, and you are once again surrounded by black darkness. Your mind swirls as you consider what you've heard and experienced. Who is Satan anyway? And if his disguise is light, is he really the opposite? Darkness?

Let's leave the hypothetical person in the pit for a moment and consider these questions. Many people today reject the idea of a devil, commonly known as Satan, because they also reject the idea of evil. After all, once we reject the Creator, we have no need for moral law, for good or evil, or for a moral lawgiver to whom we must give account. If good and evil are just constructs of society, varying from culture to culture, then why would a being exist who, as evil, would oppose God? If we have no God, we have no evil opposition. Or so some think.

But what does the Word say? It must be our guiding light.

First, we must recognize that God exists *outside of time* and that he has seen things which we can only conceive of as future events. From the start of our recorded time and history, "in the beginning" of Genesis 1:1, to the end of this age and the next, God knows, sees, and directs all events. From the time he "divided the light from the darkness" (Gen. 1:4), he knew the source of darkness (fallen Lucifer) and the source of Light (himself as Son of God).

Secondly, in Genesis 3, we read of the first sin of humankind and the consequences, *in time*. We also see a provision God made to bring that first couple back into fellowship with him. *Before time*, God knew this provision would be needed. There, in the garden, *in time*, we see the subtlety of the fallen Lucifer, who appears as a harmless serpent. I always thought it was strange that when the serpent talked to Eve, she didn't freak out and run to Adam, exclaiming, "The snake just talked to me!" I think that animal to human communication was possible before sin entered.

Also, we know that death was not yet part of their experience, because the warning was that in the day they would eat of the tree of the knowledge of good and evil (thus ruining their innocence and introducing them to what sin is and brings), they would die. Though they didn't drop dead immediately, their perfect nature and fellowship with God died. And an animal was slain to cover their nakedness and sin. Death entered.

But note how the devil tempted Eve. He appeared as a creature whom she didn't fear and most likely with whom she had conversed before. I say that because it didn't surprise her when he started talking. He didn't start right out with an accusation against God; rather, he planted a seed of doubt in her mind, a seed of suspicion about God's motives. He said, "Has God indeed said, 'You shall not eat of every tree of the garden'?" (Gen 3:1 NKJV). No doubt he was pointing her attention to the forbidden tree. Eve, in her defense of God's command, added some words, "nor shall you touch it" (v. 3 NKJV).

Then the sneaky snake got down to business. "You will not surely die: For God knows that in the day you eat of it, your eyes will be opened, and you will be like God, knowing good and evil" (Gen. 3:4-5 NKJV).

The devil planted the seed of suspicion in Eve's mind. Maybe he was right, she could have supposed. Maybe God was trying to keep her from knowing all that she could know. Maybe God was just trying to keep her and Adam subservient to him. So she looked at the fruit on the tree and saw that it was pleasant and desirable. It could make her wise. So, she ate. And gave it to Adam, who had finally showed up on the scene, and he ate.

It's interesting that the devil didn't tempt her with the fruit from the Tree of Life—promising that she would live forever or be young forever. (But then, aging—an effect of sin—had not yet entered.) The fruit from the Tree of Life was not prohibited. It truly would have been good for her. It would have honored God and led to quite a different result if eaten before sin entered. And it would have obstructed the devil's evil plan to kill, steal, and destroy.

It's also important to know that the devil didn't describe the results that would follow eating from the Tree of Knowledge of Good and Evil. He didn't say,

> You'll learn how to think for yourself and make your own way apart from God. You'll discover sensations and thrills you never dreamed of before, and you'll ruin your body and your mind with substances and excess of pleasure. You'll bring in the possibility of eternal separation from God. Oh, and by the way, you'll learn what it means to be sick, infirm, in pain, and you'll eventually die.

She wouldn't have known what all that meant anyway, especially the "die" part, because nothing had ever died yet. Animals were all vegetarian. Nothing had died, even as food. Death entered as a consequence of sin—the sin of disobedience and rebellion, the sin of pride and a desire to be like God, to be one's own god, to know evil.

Just so, when the devil lures us to the pit of darkness, he doesn't promise negative things. He offers what he cannot deliver, calling darkness "light" and evil "good." He offers us a way to be our own god, but he is a liar.

Why did God make a being that would do this to us? Didn't he know that the devil would turn out bad? Of course he did. How else would he demonstrate the life-giving, freedom-bringing light of his Son, Jesus, than as the True Light shining in the devil's darkness?

And darkness is what the devil specializes in. It is who he is. And into that darkness, the True Light continues to shine, just as it did in the beginning. The only positive thing to come out of that first sin is redemption, which was God's plan all along, even as the first prophecy hinted at in Genesis 3:15.

In Isaiah 14:12-17 we read about the devil's origin and prideful rebellion against God. Translating from *The Interlinear Bible*, we see this pronouncement:

> O Lucifer [shining star], son of the morning, how you have fallen from the heavens! You are cut down to the ground, who weakens the nations. For you have said in your heart, "I will go up to the heavens. I will raise my throne above the stars of God. And I will sit on the mount of meeting in the sides of the north. I will go up over the heights of clouds; I will be likened to the Most High." Yet you shall go down to Sheol, to the sides of the Pit [dungeon; prison]. They who see you shall stare at you, shall ponder at you: "Is this the one who made the earth tremble, shaking kingdoms, setting the world like a desert [wilderness], who tore down its cities, and did not let his prisoners loose to go home?"[1]

Lucifer, an angel created to be light, sought to be greater than God. His prideful ego sent him on a trip that insured his downfall. And he sent Eve on that same ego trip, saying in Genesis 3:5, "ye shall be as gods, knowing good and evil."

When speaking to the seventy disciples he had sent out, Jesus spoke words that show both his own eternal existence as God and God's knowledge unlimited by time. In Luke 10:18, we read, "And he [Jesus] said unto them, 'I beheld Satan as lightning fall from heaven.'" In the scope of time, we read of this event happening during the tribulation, at the end of this age of grace. See Revelation 12:3, 7-9. This speaks of a war in heaven, fought by angels, wherein, as verse 9 says, "the great dragon was cast out, that old serpent, called the Devil, and Satan, which deceiveth the whole world: he was cast out into the earth, and his angels [demons] were cast out with him."

Some might ask, "If he's in heaven now, why do we have such trouble with him on earth?" Though he is literally before the throne, accusing believers, he is also in the realm of the air, working in cultures of the world, deceiving individuals, organizations, and nations.

But how can such a horrid creature deceive anyone? Who would follow an ugly beast? Satan was created beautiful. Describing the king of Tyre in terms symbolic of the devil, Ezekiel 28:12-15 (NKJV) says this:

> *You were the seal of perfection,*
> *Full of wisdom and perfect in beauty.*
> *You were in Eden, the garden of God;*
> *Every precious stone was your covering;*
> *The sardius, topaz, and diamond,*
> *Beryl, onyx, and jasper,*
> *Sapphire, turquoise, and emerald with gold.*
> *The workmanship of your timbrels and pipes*
> *Was prepared for you on the day you were created.*
>
> *You were the anointed cherub who covers;*
> *I established you;*
> *You were on the holy mountain of God;*
> *You walked back and forth in the midst of fiery stones.*
> *You were perfect in your ways from the day you were*
>   *created,*
> *Till iniquity was found in you.*

We have already seen that the iniquity that was found in Lucifer was the sinful pride that led to rebellion: he wanted to become God.

The False Light

And isn't this the aim of rebellious, politically correct humanity today, seeking to define their own morals, to create their own heaven, to save the climate through their own human effort, and to shine in their own self-righteousness?

In Ezekiel 28:16-19, the prophet describes the judgment which would fall on Satan as though it had already happened. That's because, in the mind of God, *outside of time*, it has already happened. In Matthew 25:41, in the discussion about the judgment of the nations, we see that the "everlasting fire"—commonly known as "hell"—was "prepared for the devil and his angels." But before God sends him to that fiery eternity, God has a job for him to do.

In the New Testament, the devil is referred to by several names or titles which reflect his nature of darkness and his influence on the cultures of the world. He is called the "prince of this world" three times—in John 12:31; 14:30; and 16:11. In 2 Corinthians 4:4, he is called the "god of this world," and in Ephesians 2:2, "the prince of the power of the air," which shows his influence on the ideas of the culture. His power is the "power of darkness" (Col. 1:13), and his demons are "rulers of the darkness of this world" (Eph. 6:12). In Revelation 16:10, we see that his kingdom is "full of darkness." Earlier we saw that he refused to let his prisoners loose, and in 2 Timothy 2:25-26, we see that those who oppose God (and thereby, themselves) are caught in "the snare of the devil . . . taken captive by him at his will."

In Chapter 10 we will see who comes to set the captives free, and in Chapter 11 we will see what those who are set free can do to help others become free.

But though the devil's nature is darkness, he is a master of disguise, as we saw earlier—the strange, eerie, hypnotic light in the pit. Not only do false teachers masquerade as true, but Satan also impersonates a good angel. In discussing false teachers in 2 Corinthians 11:13-15 (MEV), Paul says,

> For such are false apostles and deceitful workers, disguising themselves as apostles of Christ. And no wonder! For even Satan disguises himself as an angel of light. Therefore it is no great thing if his ministers also disguise themselves as ministers of righteousness, whose end will be according to their works.

Why would Satan want to disguise himself? So that, just as he "deceived Eve through his trickery," he would also lead believers away from "the simplicity that is in Christ" (2 Cor. 11:3). Referring to the devil as a thief, Jesus said, "The thief does not come except to steal, and to kill, and to destroy," in contrast to Jesus' purpose, who came that we "may have life," and that we "may have it more abundantly" (John 10:10 NKJV).

The most successful criminals come masked or pretending to be someone else, camouflaging their true nature and mission. And so, we find ourselves in that pit, surrounded by darkness, enticed by false lights, and wondering what to do.

Discussion Questions

1. Discuss the reality of the devil, called Satan and other names and titles. Do you believe he exists?

2. Discuss the similarity between the first temptation in the garden and any temptation you may have faced. Do you see the subtlety of the tempter?

3. How do you answer someone who says, "Why would a good God make an evil devil?"

Personal Reflection

1. Have you ever experienced contact with false teaching, eerie people that creep you out, or a sense of terrible evil close at hand?

2. Do you believe that people can be possessed by demons? What Scriptures do you find to support that?

Verses to Consider

1. Read 1 John 3:8 and Hebrews 2:14-15.

    (a) Do you think that God planned for Satan to become lifted up with pride and to rebel against him, seeking to be his own god?

    (b) Does it seem fair that God would create the devil just so that Jesus, the Son of God, could come and die to deliver us from the devil?

    (c) Do you see that Jesus delivers us, the prisoners of the devil, when the devil himself refused to set us free?

2. Read Luke 22:53; and John 10:17-18.

(a) Do you see that people in rebellion against God can do the bidding of the devil, the prince of darkness?

(b) Though Jesus went with the Jewish officials, do you think that the enemy won that battle? Or was it supposed to happen that way?

Victory through Light

3. Read 2 Corinthians 2:17; 4:3-4; 11:3, 13-15; 2 Peter 2:1-3; and Galatians 1:6-8.

    (a) Who blinds the minds of unbelievers?

    (b) Why does he blind them?

    (c) How does he blind them?

4. Read John 8:44; Genesis 3:1; and Jude v. 6.

    (a) The devil and the angels that rebelled with him left the positions that they could have had with God. Do you think they realize what they've lost?

    (b) The devil is a liar and the father of lies. Do you see that rejecting the truth about God leads to lying, deception, and darkness?

    (c) Would you say that Satan wants to keep people blinded to the light and truth of Jesus Christ and that he uses lies and deception to keep them blinded?

5. Read Psalms 40:1-3; 143:3-11; Jeremiah 17:7; and Romans 10:9-11.

    (a) Is the devil the ultimate enemy, motivating all others who are against us?

    (b) When we feel like we have been pushed down into a pit of darkness and despair, to whom should we call for help? Will he help?

(c) Is believing the truth about Jesus Christ the way to truth and light?

CHAPTER 10

†

The True Light

IN THE PREVIOUS CHAPTER we saw the "prince of darkness" masquerading as light. In this chapter, we will see the True Light in whom is no darkness. Let's return to our hypothetical pit:

You look up, away from the dark pit, the name of Jesus on your tongue.

High, high above you glows a tiny pinprick of light. It grows closer and larger and brighter. A voice speaks with loving authority, "I am the light of the world. He who follows Me shall not walk in darkness, but have the light of life" (John 8:12 NKJV).

You struggle against the invisible walls of the pit. You can't climb out. You jump up and down, but you cannot gain the height you need to clear the opening of the pit. You want that light, but you cannot attain to it. Despair and desperation fill your mind and heart. But there is no way out. No way to get to that light, to that wonderful voice, to that promise of life.

Feeling the darkness swirl around you like a vortex sucking you down, your mind reels: "Uncountable evils surround me; my mistakes are gripping my soul so that I can't look up. They are more than the hairs on my head; my heart dies within me. Please, O LORD, deliver me. O LORD, hurry to help me. I cannot get out."[1] You open your mouth to scream. Only a whisper comes out: "Jesus, rescue me."

Suddenly your feet are on a solid rock with solid ground all around you. Light enfolds you. Behind you there is only a shadow of the pit that was, but it has no pull on you now.

You step toward the light's source. You can see! Everything around you is clear. You draw in a deep breath of fresh air and sigh, "Thank you, Jesus."

Whether you emerged from the pit as a believer who was led astray and entrapped by our culture (under the influence of the devil) or as a first-time responder to Christ, you are free from the darkness. Free. By simply calling on the name of Jesus to be saved.[2] Jesus is the light that lightens our darkness, just as he said in John 8:12: "I am the light of the world. He who follows Me shall not walk in darkness, but have the light of life" (NKJV). Light and life are connected from the beginning in the Word of God. In John 1:1-5 (MEV), we read concerning Jesus,

> In the beginning was the Word, and the Word was with God, and Word was God. He was in the beginning with God. All things were created through Him, and without Him nothing was created that was created. In Him was life, and the life was the light of mankind. The light shines in darkness, but the darkness has not overcome it.

John the Baptist was sent to prepare the way for this Light, which is "The true Light, which enlightens everyone" as John says in John 1:9 (MEV). However, though the light is available to all, not all receive it. Some refuse to believe. But to those who believe in Jesus and receive his light, great blessing follows. John says, "Yet to all

The True Light

who received Him, He gave the power to become sons of God, to those who believed in His name" (John 1:12 MEV). As we've studied before—simple faith in Jesus Christ, not performance of works—leads to new life in Christ as children of God.

To that person who believes, even the tiniest spark of the glorious light of the gospel will rip open the darkness and cause the shadows to flee. It is in that first ray of light that we often must make a choice. Do we shield our eyes from it, turn away, and choose darkness? Or do we run to the light, embrace it, and walk in it? In 1 Peter 2:9, the apostle Peter says that we are called out of darkness into God's marvelous light. That brings up an interesting question.

Who would choose to remain in or return to darkness? King Solomon tells us in Proverbs 2:13 that evil persons "leave the paths of uprightness, to walk in the ways of darkness." He says in Ecclesiastes 2:13, "Then I saw that wisdom excelleth folly, as far as light excelleth darkness." His conclusion, then, is that it is wiser to walk in light, in uprightness (morally honorable, straight, doing what is right) than to walk in darkness (which is folly).

Jesus explains this difference in John 3: 19-21 (MEV). After telling us that he came to save, not condemn, the world, and that belief in him transfers a person from condemnation to salvation, he explains,

> This is the verdict, that light has come into the world, and men loved darkness rather than light, because their deeds were evil. For everyone who does evil hates the light and does not come to the light, lest his deeds should be exposed. But he who does the truth comes to the light, that it may be revealed that his deeds have been done in God.

Thus, the choice is between light and dark, good and evil, wisdom and folly. We should be glad we were pulled from the pit by the love and grace of God, "who commanded light to shine out of darkness, who has shone in our hearts to give the light of the knowledge of the glory of God in the face of Jesus Christ" (2 Cor. 4:6 NKJV).

Life and light are connected in other verses in the Bible also. In Psalm 36:9, David declares, "For with You is the fountain of life: in Your light shall we see light" (NKJV). Psalm 119:130 says, "The entrance of Your words gives light; It gives understanding to the simple" (NKJV), and Psalm 119:105 says, "Your word is a lamp to my feet And a light to my path" (NKJV). Physically and spiritually, we do need light to guide our path. We need it to know what is around us, to see where we are going, and to discern the pitfalls that would cause us to stumble.

In Acts 26:23, Paul shared with Festus and King Agrippa a prophecy of Moses that was fulfilled in Christ: "That Christ should suffer, and that he should be the first that should rise from the dead, and should shew light unto the people, and to the Gentiles." Festus proclaimed Paul crazy, and King Agrippa said, (v. 28 author paraphrase): "You almost persuade me to be a Christian." Almost isn't good enough, though.

C. S. Lewis wrote, "I believe in Christianity as I believe that the sun has risen: not only because I see it, but because by it I see everything else."[3] We can't look directly at the sun for very long, even in sunglasses, though we can watch the sunrise. By it we see our surroundings with ever increasing clarity. Likewise, through biblical Christianity we can see everything else in life. Every aspect of our life lines up and becomes clear when our focus is on Jesus Christ and his teachings. When the light shines upon us, we must accept it, or the darkness will sweep us away.

I think of that young team of soccer players who were trapped in a cave under a mountain for two weeks—twelve teens and their coach. Total darkness, except when they could use their torches (flashlights) and when the rescuers brought lights down. With the cave flooding and more rain coming, it must have been like being in a pit, such as we've imagined in this book. But they had each other to encourage them and a coach to teach them how to relax. They were not each alone in a dark pit with no way out.

Their escape was not sudden, as in our release from the metaphorical pit. When they got out, they traveled through dark passageways, some that were under water. They were with rescuers who knew the way out and how to get them out. Because the rescue was successful, though one former Thai Navy Seal perished, this event is a symbol of hope and patience, of people coming together to help one another.

However, had the boys each struck out in different directions trying to find their own way in the dark labyrinth of passageways, they would have perished in the murky water underground. With decreasing oxygen levels, had they panicked and not followed the directions of the coach, and later the rescuers, it would have been quite a different symbol.

It would have then represented our culture today where people weave through the darkness from idea to idea, from cause to cause, from human leader to human leader, never coming into the light of truth. From relativism to tolerance to intolerance of Christians; from a woman's right to kill her pre-born child to open borders and open bathrooms; from homosexual advocates to those seeking to normalize pedophilia: Tunnel after tunnel, passageway after passageway, an endless struggle in ever darkening darkness.

But as we have seen in this chapter, there is hope. There is a way out, just as there was a way out for those Thai teens. For us as individuals and for our families and culture, Jesus stands ready to deliver. He himself went into the darkness to bring us into the light, just as those divers did. He took our place and was cut off from his Father. When darkness abounded, he gave his life. But he rose from the tomb—alive and glorified. And the Light shone and still shines today.

He is the Light that lifts us out of darkness. All we have to do is call on him, as is written in Romans 10:13: "For whosoever shall call upon the name of the Lord shall be saved." Additionally, included in that term "be saved" is to be set free from the prison of darkness. Isaiah prophesied about this in several places, but in Isaiah 42:6-7, he speaks of Christ being given "for a light . . . to open the blind eyes, to bring out the prisoners from the prison, and them that sit in darkness out of the prison house." This prophecy is quoted in Matthew 4:16 and Luke 1:79, regarding Jesus.

Notice, he brings us out of darkness. He delivers us from the prison house—from whatever prison we have made for ourselves or gotten ourselves into. Whatever pit we've fallen into, he lifts us out. We cannot get out on our own.

I have heard of people who kicked various addictions through their own willpower. It's admirable if one can do that. Most can't. But even then, the deep emotional wounds that led to the addiction remain. Only Jesus can heal those and lift the individual out of the dark prison of their past where the emotional wounds were received. Psalm 107:10, 13-14 (NKJV) make this clear:

> *Those who sat in darkness and in the shadow of death,*
> *Bound in affliction and irons—*
> *. . . cried out to the LORD in their trouble,*
> *And He saved them out of their distresses.*
> *He brought them out of darkness and the shadow of death,*
> *And broke their chains in pieces.*

Additionally, Isaiah 9:2 prophesies of the Messiah, Jesus, "The people that walked in darkness have seen a great light: they that dwell in the land of the shadow of death, upon them hath the light shined." This is the same chapter with the prophecy often quoted at Christmas: "For unto us a child is born, unto us a son is given: and the government shall be upon his shoulder: and his name shall be called, 'Wonderful, Counsellor, The mighty God, The everlasting Father, the Prince of Peace'" (Isa. 9:6).

The True Light

Surely, Jesus is the Light, and he delivers us from darkness, even as the psalmist declares, "The LORD my God will enlighten my darkness," and in another place, "God is the LORD; And He has given us light" (Pss. 18:28; 118:27 NKJV).

Discussion Questions

1. Have you experienced the kind of deliverance from spiritual darkness discussed in the first part of this chapter?

2. Discuss what you know about the Thai soccer team cave experience. If you need additional information, google it or go to https://www.bbc.com/news/world-asia-44791998. What other lessons can you draw from their experience? What do you think would have happened if they had tried to get themselves out? Was it necessary and fortunate that others went into the darkness to get them?

3. Discuss how Jesus can lift us from spiritual darkness and physical darkness.

Personal Reflection

1. Has the Lord given you light? Do you see him as the light in a dark world?

2. If you think about the messages that you receive from our media, entertainment industry, and political factions, would you say that "buying into" their messages would bring light? Or does it bring darkness?

3. Have you ever experienced a run-in with a dark spirit or force? Did you call out to the Lord at that time? I remember a time in my rebellious years when I went home with a guy to his apartment above a store building. When he pulled out a pistol and ordered me to take off my clothes, I ran. At the doorway, I heard him yell, "Get back here or I will shoot you." All the way down the stairs I called on Jesus to save me, promising to never get drunk again. I didn't keep my end of the bargain at that time, but God kept me from getting shot. Later, I realized what a dark force I had dealt with and how God surely kept me.

Verses to Consider

1. Read Psalm 40:1-5 and 43:3.

    (a) Can David's cheer of victory and deliverance be yours? Note that David cried out and the LORD heard his cry.

    (b) Are light and truth connected? Can they really lead you in your daily life?

    (c) What does coming to God's "holy hill," and to his "tabernacle" mean? Does it mean you have to go to church? Does it mean you have to clean up your life? Or does it mean that you embrace the Lord and his righteousness, accept the deliverance and salvation he has provided, and let him lead you to a fellowship of believers with whom you can grow?

2. Read Joel 2:32; Romans 10:13; and Acts 2:21.

The True Light

   (a) Is calling on the name of the Lord really enough to be delivered from darkness and death?

   (b) Does faith in him have to be the motivation of calling on his name?

3. Read Isaiah 61:1-2 and Luke 4:16-21.

   (a) To whom does this prophecy in Isaiah refer?

   (b) Is the "opening of the prison" like being lifted from the pit?

   (c) Is this deliverance a spiritual one or a physical pardon for political prisoners?

   (d) Does Jesus promise spiritual deliverance to whosoever asks?

4. Read Acts 26:13-18; 1 Peter 2:9; 2 Corinthians 5:21; and Ephesians 5:8.

   (a) Saul's name was changed to Paul during his early ministry. Before the incident described in Acts 26 took place, Saul persecuted Christians, often to death. He imprisoned many and even gave assent to the stoning of Stephen, as seen in Acts 7 and 8:1. Once Saul's eyes were opened and he was delivered from darkness to light, his calling was to open eyes of Jews and Gentiles and "to turn them from darkness to light, and from the power of Satan unto God" (Acts 26:18). Is this what Peter was talking about when he wrote that believers should sing the praises of God who had called them "out of darkness into his marvellous light" (1 Peter 2:9)?

Victory through Light

(b) Do you see that being in that light brings forgiveness of sins?

(c) What do you think is the inheritance that Paul speaks of in Acts 26:18? Is it earthly wealth or a heavenly inheritance?

(d) In Acts 26:18, Paul also mentions them being "sanctified by faith" in Jesus. What does being sanctified mean? Could it be related to shining as light to others, just as Christ was light to us? (Hint: in this verse "sanctified" is the Greek word that means "to make holy; to purify or consecrate.") Does the faith in Christ that brings deliverance and forgiveness also make us holy in God's sight? And if we believers are what 2 Corinthians 5:21 says we are—the "righteousness of God" in Christ, then ought we to shine as lights to the world?

5. Read 1 Timothy 1:12-16.

  (a) When Saul persecuted the church, he did it "ignorantly in unbelief" (1 Tim. 1:13). When we do what society says rather than what the Word says, are we doing it ignorantly or in unbelief?

  (b) Since Saul/Paul was given a ministry after his conversion, can we expect to have a ministry according to what God desires of us by his grace?

  (c) Paul became a pattern for future believers. Can we be patterns to those coming after us?

CHAPTER 11

†

Children of Light

WE ARE CALLED INTO LIGHT, and what a glorious calling it is! Paraphrasing into today's English,

> But you are a chosen offspring, a royal priesthood, a holy nation, a purchased people, that you should speak out the excellence, virtue, and praise of him who has called you out of darkness into His marvellous light. (1 Peter 2:9)

Let us think back a moment to how unsettled and unsure we felt in that dark pit. Even if we back up to the time before we stepped off that curb, to the time we simply were surrounded by darkness, or to the time when the shadows lengthened and darkened around us and we began to hear those frightful footsteps, the sounds of the enemy moving around us . . . did we long for light?

Have you ever driven in fog so dense you could only see about five yards ahead? Have you ever driven on an unfamiliar country road on a night when thick clouds hid the moon and stars so that you had no natural light, and your headlights (even on bright) were glowing dimly, as a result of a dying alternator or dirty headlight covers? I have, and I found it very unsettling. Especially when we lose sense of direction, times like that can cause us to wish for light. We get a sense of how much we need light.

This is equally true in the spiritual realm. Our culture has morally lost its way and has placed bad over good, and wrong over right. It prizes political correctness over the Word of God, and it puts sin over righteousness. Amid this, we are left to spiritually navigate familiar and unfamiliar roads without a compass, light, or map. Into this darkness shines "the light of the glorious gospel of Christ, who is the image of God" (2 Cor. 4:4).

The God of creation shines the light of Christ into our darkness. Paul tells us, "For it is the God who commanded light to shine out of darkness, who has shone in our hearts to give the light of the knowledge of the glory of God in the face of Jesus Christ" (2 Cor. 4:6 NKJV). And seeing that light and believing, we are lifted "out of darkness" into that wonderful light. However, we are not set there to just vegetate.

God has a purpose for us in his light. That light represents the spiritual presence of God in us. The darkness represents the spirit of the world and the antichrist. Thus, because we are in the light, we also have a spiritual purpose—a duty to dispel the darkness. Paul says in 1 Corinthians 2:12, "Now we have received, not the spirit of the world, but the Spirit who is from God, that we might know the things that have been freely given to us by God" (NKJV). These things include spiritual blessings—eternal life and a commission to share the light.

Being delivered from the darkness, we are set free from the power of darkness. Paul writes in Colossians 1:13-14, "He has delivered us from the power of darkness and conveyed us into the kingdom of the Son of His love, in whom we have redemption through His blood, the forgiveness of sins" (NKJV). Redemption and forgiveness are two things we have been freely given by God.

Redemption means we have been bought out of the slave market never to be sold again. Forgiveness of sins means that whatever bad thing we've done or will do has been cast as far as the east is from the west, so that God will not bring it up to us ever again. Those two things are phenomenal benefits of being delivered from darkness into His light, from the *power* of darkness into his kingdom (family).

However, because we are still on earth, in this world though not of it, we are not totally free of the *presence* of darkness in our culture. The epitome of darkness is the devil, and he seeks to devour us by whatever means he can. We read in 1 Peter 5:8-9, "Be sober, be vigilant; because your adversary the devil, walks about like a roaring lion, seeking whom he may devour. Resist him, steadfast in the faith" (NKJV).

Resisting the devil involves eight areas of the active work of God in us. These eight areas enable us to praise him who has delivered us from the immediate darkness and from its power, and who will one day deliver us from its presence.

God's Active Work #1: Fight the Spiritual Battle

Since the devil is on the offence, "seeking whom he may devour" (1 Peter 5:8), the first area of God's active work in us is that of spiritual battle. In 2 Timothy 4:7, Paul speaks of having "fought a good fight," and in 2 Timothy 2:3, he encourages Timothy (and us) to "endure hardness, as a good soldier of Jesus Christ." In 1 Timothy 1:18, he tells Timothy (and us) to "war a good warfare."

But what kind of fight and what kind of war does he refer to? Definitely not a physical one such as the crusades or purges of the dark ages. Paul makes it clear that we fight a spiritual battle, "Holding faith and a good conscience" (1 Tim. 1:19). We cling to the Word of God and the truth that has set us free. We walk in obedience to the love of God so that our conscience is clear. We battle spirits in a war of ideas as we "earnestly contend for the faith" (Jude v. 3).

In his letter to the Ephesians, Paul describes this warfare and our weapons and attire:

> Finally, my brothers, be strong in the Lord and in the power of his might. Put on the whole armor of God that you may be able to stand against the schemes of the devil. For our fight is not against flesh and blood, but against principalities, against powers, against the rulers of the darkness of this world, and against spiritual forces of evil in the heavenly places. Therefore take up the whole armor of God that you may be able to resist in the evil day, and having done all, to stand. Stand therefore, having your waist girded with truth, having put on the breastplate of righteousness, having your feet fitted with the readiness of the gospel of peace, and above all, taking the shield of faith, with which you will be able to extinguish all the fiery arrows of the evil one. Take the helmet of salvation and the sword of the Spirit, which is the word of God.
>
> Pray in the Spirit always with all kinds of prayer and supplication. To that end be alert with all perseverance and supplication for all the saints [believers]. (Eph. 6:10-18 MEV)

According to that Scripture, we battle spiritual forces, including doubts and fears with which the enemy would try to cripple us. Thus, we need to know the Word and be equipped in how to use it to quench those doubts and fears. We need to know the truth, to wear God's righteousness, and to be ready to share the gospel of peace. And we wield the sword of the Spirit, the Word of God, as a light sabre to defeat the foes of darkness and deception.

In Chapter 9, we saw that the devil and his host of fallen angels accuse us before God in heaven, and that he and they will be cast out of heaven in the realm of time, not too long from now. Many of his demons wander the earth now, persuading people to do horrible things to others. Against these, we must stand in battle dress, praying always, interceding for others, and staying alert.

In 2 Corinthians 10:3-6 (MEV), Paul discusses the enemy further, showing that our battle is with the false ideas and perversions of the devil and his host, not against them physically. Many of us never encounter a demon or are called upon to cast out a demon. But we are all called to combat the urges that spring from demonic spirits and the ideas spawned by the devil:

> For though we walk in the flesh [body], we do not war according to the flesh. For the weapons of our warfare are not carnal, but mighty through God to the pulling down of strongholds, casting down imaginations and every high thing that exalts itself against the knowledge of God, bringing every thought into captivity to the obedience of Christ.

Thus, we engage in a battle of spirits, a war of ideas. To do so, we must "cast off the works of darkness and . . . put on the armor of light" (Rom. 13:12).

God's Active Work #2: Choose Not to Sin

Notice that putting on the armor of light (which is described in detail in Ephesians 6, quoted above) follows "cast[ing] off the works of darkness." We looked at some of those works in detail in Chapter 7. Basically, anything that doesn't glorify God, line up with the Word, or shine with his light can be considered a work of darkness. If we can't do a deed in Jesus' name or do it heartily as unto him, then it shouldn't be done.[1] Too restrictive? Just the contrary. This liberates us to be all that God wants us to be, to grow in him as he desires, and to receive all the blessings he has for us, including the reward of the inheritance.

The works of darkness are the works of the flesh. We are to refrain from those and can only do so as we yield to the Lord. Peter discusses these works a few verses after he tells us that we are called out of darkness into God's marvelous light. He shows that we still must resist the presence of darkness in our lives because of our old "human" nature. He says, "Beloved, I beg you as sojourners and pilgrims, abstain from fleshly lusts which war against the soul" (1 Peter 2:11 NKJV). He reminds us that earth is not our final home, that we are headed to heaven, and that while here, we should refuse to engage in sinful things that temporarily satisfy lusts but bring about spiritual loss and damage, as well as other detrimental consequences.

See Colossians 3:5 and also Ephesians 5:1-4, 11, which states plainly, "And have no fellowship with the unfruitful works of darkness, but rather reprove them" (v. 11). To reprove or abstain from these lusts, we must yield wholly to the Lord. This is the second area of God's active work in us: we must choose not to sin.

God's Active Work #3: Don't Conform to the World

We find the key to our part in this in Romans 12:1-2:

> I beseech you therefore, brethren, by the mercies of God, that you present your bodies a living sacrifice, holy, acceptable to God, which is your reasonable service. And do not be conformed to this world, but be transformed by the renewing of your mind, that you may prove what is that good and acceptable and perfect will of God. (NKJV)

Presenting ourselves to God for him to make of us what he wants is a way we have of truly serving him. And it is logical and reasonable to do so.

The second part of doing that is to not be conformed to this world, to its culture of darkness, political correctness, and false worldviews. That is the third active work of God in us. Jesus prayed for us, saying,

> I have given them Your word; and the world has hated them because they are not of the world, just as I am not of the world. I do not pray that You should take them out of the world, but that You should keep them from the evil one. They are not of the world, just as I am not of the world. Sanctify them by Your truth. Your word is truth. (John 17:14-17 NKJV)

That he was speaking of all believers for all time is obvious from verse 20, where he includes "those who will believe in Me through their word" (NKJV).

Not being of the world means that we let the truth establish us, as to our beliefs and conduct. We do not compromise with the vain philosophies of our time. We reject moral relativism, pluralism, syncretism (the attempt to make all beliefs the same; the "all-roads-lead-to-heaven" fallacy), postmodernism, and political correctness as a standard of righteousness. We reject the false lights of legality, self-righteousness, works, and pleasure-seeking. John sums this up in his first epistle:

> Do not love the world or the things in the world. If anyone loves the world, the love of the Father is not in him. For all that is in the world—the lust of the flesh, the lust of the eyes, and the pride of life—is not of the Father but is of the world. And the world is passing away, and the lust of it; but he who does the will of God abides forever. (1 John 2:15-17 NKJV)

We must reject the dark cocoon of the world and its ideas and let ourselves be wrapped in God's light, love, and Word, so that we can change into what God wants us to be. And in the same way that the Creator controls and directs the butterfly's emergence from the cocoon, he guides our changed lives as we turn from the ugliness of sin to the beauty of his holiness.

God's Active Work #4: Be Transformed and Renewed

So then, as we refuse to conform to the world, we are free to be transformed by the renewing of our minds. And how are our minds renewed? By the Word of God. By knowing Jesus. Renewal of our minds is the fourth active work of God in us. Having "put off the old nature with its deeds," we are to "embrace [put on] the new nature, which is renewed in knowledge after the image of Him that created it," as Paul tells us in Colossians 3:9-10 (MEV). Peter says to "grow in grace, and in the knowledge of our Lord and Savior Jesus Christ" (2 Peter 3:18).

See 1 Thessalonians 5:5-8 for a summary of our transformation from night to day, darkness to light, spiritual drunkenness and slumber to spiritual sobriety and alertness. In Acts 17:11, Paul commends the Berean believers in that "they received the word with all eagerness [readiness of mind], daily examining the Scriptures, to find out if these things were so" (MEV). Their minds were eager and ready to learn, but they searched through the Scriptures to be sure that the preaching was true and sound doctrine. This is how we find ourselves transformed, and by such transformation, we prove that God's will is good, acceptable, and perfect.

God's Active Work #5: Be Established in the Word

Becoming transformed includes becoming established in the truth of the gospel. We learn from Acts 20:32 and John 17:17 that the Word builds us up and purifies us because it is truth. It is the "present truth" in which we are to be established, as Peter speaks of in 2 Peter 1:12. And, after warning the Ephesians to avoid behaving like unbelievers, who practiced "every kind of impurity with greediness," Paul exhorts,

> But you did not learn about Christ in this manner, If indeed you have heard Him and have been taught by Him, as the truth is in Jesus: that you put off the former way of life in the old nature, which is corrupt according to the deceitful lusts, and be renewed in the spirit of your mind; and that you put on the new nature, which was created according to God in righteousness and true holiness. (Eph. 4:20-24 MEV)

It comes back to that renewal of the mind. This is not a mental exercise or learning by rote. It is a spiritual learning. It encompasses both the mind and heart. The truth establishes the mind and God's grace establishes the heart, so that our thinking is clear and our emotions are pure.

However, becoming established, the fifth active work of God in us, is not something we can do on our own. It's not a work that we must perform in order to become or remain a child of God, a believer in Jesus. It's a work that God does in us as we study and believe his Word and let his Spirit work in us. Paul gives this guarantee in 2 Thessalonians 3:3: "But the Lord is faithful, who will establish you and guard you from the evil one" (MEV).

Moreover, in Hebrews 13:9, Paul says that "it is a good thing that the heart be strengthened with grace" (MEV). In 2 Corinthians 1:21, Paul proclaims, "Now He who establishes us with you in Christ and has anointed us is God" (MEV). See also 1 Thessalonians 3:13 and 2 Thessalonians 2:17.

By his grace, God establishes us in his truth, as Jesus prayed, "Sanctify them through thy truth: thy word is truth" (John 17:17).

God's Active Work #6: Walk in the Light

While we learn and become established in the Word of truth and of his grace, we are to walk in his light as children of light—the sixth active work of God in us. When he delivers us from that dark pit, we stand in his light and can move forward in that light. Ephesians 5:8 says, "For you were once darkness, but now you are light in the Lord. Walk as children of light" (NKJV). If we fail to walk in his light and we turn back to the darkness, our path will be fraught with danger.

Jesus says, "Walk while you have the light, lest darkness overtake you; he who walks in darkness does not know where he is going" (John 12:35 NKJV). In John 8:12, Jesus says, "I am the light of the world. He who follows Me shall not walk in darkness, but have the light of life" (NKJV).

The prophet Isaiah exhorts the house of Jacob to "walk in the light of the LORD" (Isa. 2:5 NKJV). First John 1:7 lists two benefits of walking in the light: Christian fellowship and continued experience of forgiveness. Both come from unbroken fellowship with God.

God's Active Work #7: Live in the Light

If we walk in the light, we will be living in the light, which is God's seventh active work in us. When we live in the light, we have no darkness and no gray areas. To live in the light is to acknowledge that

- There is a God who created all that is. He is all-knowing, all-powerful, and ever-present.
- He longs to have a relationship with us so much that before he created the world, he devised a plan whereby we could spend eternity with him.

- Although sin separates us from him, we can have that eternal relationship with him by accepting the sacrifice of his Son, Jesus Christ, by embracing the Savior as personally ours.
- By accepting the death, burial, and resurrection of Jesus for us, we accept him into our heart and are born-again; we acknowledge that his righteousness is ours by faith, and we, thus, enter an eternal realm of life and light.
- Clothed in God's righteousness by faith in Jesus Christ, we have the power and responsibility to live a righteous life, possible only as we yield to Christ in us, putting aside our old nature (which is darkness) and living the new nature life (which is light).

In stark contrast to this, living in darkness is to claim that

- There is no God or Creator, and that all we see, hear, touch, smell, and taste came about by accident, the result of an explosion that spun the universe into existence out of nothing.
- We are no more than a slime ball evolved to the current form of human being, just like every other life form evolved (by chance or by survival of the fittest) into what it is, with odds so phenomenal as to defy our imagination or calculation.
- Being an evolved slime ball, there is no grand and noble purpose for our lives and no meaning other than chance occurrences and self-indulgence, though we may seek meaning and purpose in *causes*, which vary with the times.
- As an evolved animal, we are accountable to no one (not even to law enforcement if we live in a progressive liberal USA community).
- There is no eternal life—when we die, we're dead, so it doesn't matter what we do in this life.

Thus, our origin is dark, our history is dark, our present is dark, and our future is dark. For what is as dark as a closed coffin under six feet of soil with no hope of eternal light?

However, people in darkness want to believe they have some light. Some of them look for decency, morality, or goodness in themselves, or for some purpose or meaning outside of themselves. Many unbelievers live decent and good lives. Many unbelievers help others. If everyone followed the teachings of Jesus or even the principles of Confucius, for example, there would be no family breakdown and no civil unrest.

Unfortunately, people, by their nature, will not be at peace with one another for very long. The old human nature is darkness, being marred by sin. And no amount of thinking otherwise will change that.

Those who reject a creator God and Christ as Savior may think that everyone goes to a "better place" after this life, but if there is no God and no Creator, why would there be a spiritual life beyond this one? A "better place" to go to? If naturalistic evolution is correct, then there is no "after this life." The darkness of the grave is all we have to look forward to. Hence, the unbeliever must construct "vain philosophies" to bring hope into their existence.

Some in darkness are tricked into thinking that the false lights of relativism, tolerance, political correctness, plurality, and the postmodern worldview are real light. Others may be deceived into thinking that darkness is light, that evil spirits are friends, and that the devil is their god. It is a fact that there are Satan worshippers. There are covens of witches who cast spells, hold séances to speak to dead people, and perform other demonic acts. There are earth worshippers, who worship the created world instead of the Creator. There are humanists who believe that man can control nature and be his own god, either collectively or individually.

These are falsehoods that come from and lead to the dark pit. How much better to live in the light, surrounded by truth, love, peace, grace, hope, and all the blessings of God,

> Who hath saved us, and called us with an holy calling, not according to our works, but according to his own purpose and grace, which was given us in Christ Jesus before the world began, But is now made manifest by the appearing of our Savior Jesus Christ, who hath abolished death, and hath brought life and immortality to light through the gospel. (2 Tim. 1:9-10)

The light of the gospel brings life to those who believe. But what of those who believe, but are later deceived by the darkness of the culture? Is there any hope for them?

Absolutely! The culture cannot negate what God has done in saving us. In Job 33:28-30, we read words that reveal this faithfulness of God in bringing us from the pit: "He will deliver my soul from going into the Pit, and my life shall see the light. Lo, all of these things God often works for man, to rescue his soul from the Pit, to be enlightened with the light of the living" (author paraphrase).[2]

Living in light simply means living in the Lord. The psalmist declares, "The LORD is my light and my salvation; whom shall I fear? The LORD is the strength of my life; of whom shall I be afraid?" and "For with thee is the fountain of life: in thy light shall we see light" (Psalms 27:1 and 36:9, respectively). This is what Jesus speaks of in John 15:4, where he says, "Abide in me, and I in you." Since Jesus is that True Light, if we abide in him, we abide in light, and if he abides in us, that light abides in us. In so abiding, then, we will be living in the light.

God's Active Work #8: Be Light to Others

Finally, if we live in the light, then we will be light to others, the eighth active work of God in us. As "children of light" (John 12:36), we are to "be blameless and harmless [sincere], the sons of God, without rebuke, in the midst of a crooked and perverse nation [generation], among whom ye shine as lights in the world;

Holding forth the word of life" (Phil. 2:15-16). His light shines in us to give light to others. Jesus speaks of this in Matthew 5:14-16:

> You are the light of the world. A city that is set on a hill cannot be hidden. Nor do they light a lamp and put it under a basket, but on a lampstand, and it gives light to all who are in the house. Let your light so shine before men, that they may see your good works and glorify your Father in heaven. (NKJV)

Our good works—the works that God does in us and enables us to do for others—bring light to those in darkness.

We see this explained in Proverbs 4:18-19: "But the path of the just is as the shining light that shineth more and more unto the perfect day. The way of the wicked is as darkness: they know not at what they stumble." Because we are free from the darkness and are blessed with the light, let us be light to others, even as Paul says, "For you were once darkness, but now you are light in the Lord. Walk as children of light" (Eph. 5:8 NKJV). He affirms this in 1 Thessalonians 5:5: "Ye are all the children of light, and the children of the day: we are not of the night, nor of darkness."

What better purpose in life could there be than to be children of light, walking and living in the True Light of Jesus Christ, and being light to those in darkness?

Discussion Questions

1. Discuss the reality that we are called into light and free from the power of darkness but are still subject to its presence among us. Do you see the presence of darkness in our society? How about in your own life and family?

2. List and discuss the eight tasks we have in combatting the presence of darkness.

Personal Reflection

1. Do you agree with the description of what the nonbeliever thinks about life?

2. Do you think it's possible to live in both realms at the same time—darkness and light?

3. Do you believe you have been called into light and set free from the power of darkness?

Verses to Consider

1. Read John 8:12; Ephesians 5:8; Matthew 5:14-16; 1 Thessalonians 5:5; and Philippians 2:14-16.

   (a) What is the relationship between Jesus as Light and believers as light?

   (b) Do believers have a responsibility to shine light into a dark world?

2. Read 1 Corinthians 9:24-27 and 2 Timothy 2:4-7.

   (a) What other metaphors for our "warfare" does Paul use to make it clear that our faith should be an active pursuit of truth?

   (b) Keep in mind that Paul's words "lest . . . I should be a castaway" do not mean that he would lose salvation, but that he would fail to qualify for the full inheritance of heaven—his reward would be less than it could have been.

Do you want to have God's best—the gold medal? Or will you settle for just getting a participation trophy, as it were?

3. Read Colossians 3:1—4:6; Ephesians 4:17—5:7; and Galatians 5:19-25.

    (a) These portions contrast the old nature with the new nature and show the deeds done by each. Do you understand the difference between the old nature and the new nature?

    (b) Can you find other verses that also show this contrast?

    (c) With 2 Corinthians 5:17 in mind, do you see that we have been set free from the old nature and have been given a new nature by faith in Jesus Christ? This is not a work we can do. Jesus has done it for us when he lifted us from the pit of darkness and placed us in his marvelous light, making us children of light. Does that truth thrill you?

CHAPTER 12

†

Triumph of Light

SO HERE WE ARE, FREE from darkness, walking and living in light, being light for others. But all around us, we still see the darkness of our culture. Relative morality still thrives; pluralism continues to be praised; and academia silences Christians. We are told to privatize our faith so we don't offend anyone, and we're taken to court if we stand for biblical principles of godliness in our businesses. Postmodern lack of reason and meaning flourishes; and political correctness is the order of the day, with its new rules and absolutes. Let's face it. Our culture is growing darker and darker.

In the early 1980s, I saw the darkness growing and thought the end was near. Here it is now, some thirty-five years later, give or take a few, and society is still ticking away, growing darker. Television and movies show things I would have never expected in the 1980s. Public schools approach education in a way I never foresaw. I knew that things were a mess, politically, when the first President Bush announced the beginning of "a new world order." I saw red flags and heard distress signals.

The new world order is exactly what the kingdom of darkness is about: all the societies of the world being manipulated, engineered, and managed by a group of people who have rejected the light of Jesus Christ and the knowledge of God. And most deceptive about the new world order is that certain denominations, self-identifying as Christian, go along with it and work to usher it in.

Collectively, humanity stands where we stood near the end of Chapter 1—on the precipice of that dark pit, surrounded by darkness, feeling the absence of light. We are not far from the time of total darkness, when judgment will fall, according to the Scriptures. That judgment period is often referred to as the tribulation[1], the time of Jacob's trouble (Jer. 30:7), and as the day of wrath[2] in several Scriptures.

I don't intend here to discuss prophecy in detail or to speculate about the exact date these end-time events will begin to unfold. Some people will scoff and say that people have been saying that since the first century A.D. (See 2 Peter 3:4.) They mock the end time, especially since "of that day and hour no one knows, not even the angels in heaven, nor the Son, but only the Father" (Mark 13:32 NKJV). All I can say to that is that the signs are present now, more than they ever have been. I prefer to live as though the time is near, rather than to hide my head in the sand and be caught off-guard. I have tucked my head in the sand before, so to speak, and have found that it is dark under the sand.

I have learned that believers who live in the light also live in expectation of the fulfillment of end-time prophecy. Peter emphasizes this in his second epistle, wherein he declares prophecy to be more certain than even his experience with Jesus on the Mount of Transfiguration. In that event, Jesus shone with glory, and the Father announced from heaven his approval of his Son. In addition to that wonderful experience, Peter says,

> We have also a more sure word of prophecy, whereunto ye do well that ye take heed, as unto a light that shineth in a dark place, until the day dawn, and the day star arise in your hearts: Knowing this first, that no prophecy of the scripture is of any private interpretation. For the prophecy came not in old time by the will of man: but holy men of God spake as they were moved by the Holy Ghost. (2 Peter 1:19-21)

Thus, prophecy is a more sure word than even our testimony or experience as believers. And prophecy points to a coming darkness, followed by the triumph of light.

With all this coming darkness, should we just stop trying to shine? God forbid. Pastor Greg Laurie mentioned at the 2018 Harvest SoCal, "Light shines brighter when things are really dark."[3] The light we shine into the darkness will pierce the darkness with the truth of the gospel of Christ. The "one more" that we can illuminate, who will accept Jesus as Savior before the judgment, will be worth the contempt, criticism, scorn, and ridicule that we experience. After all, Christians in some lands endure outright persecution and death for their faith in Christ. But beheaded or burnt, their light shines on.

The Bible tells us that the days will become darker and darker. Joel describes it as, "A day of darkness and of gloominess, a day of clouds and of thick darkness" (Joel 2:2). Calling it "the great day of the Lord," Zephaniah declares, "That day is a day of wrath, a day of trouble and distress, a day of wasteness and desolation, a day of darkness and gloominess, a day of clouds and thick darkness" (Zeph. 1:14, 15). Though this refers to spiritual darkness, there will also be a literal darkness during that time. This physical darkness occurs after the ranks of the church are raptured, when the Antichrist appears to rule over the earth:

> And the fifth angel poured out his vial upon the seat of the beast; and his kingdom was full of darkness; and they

gnawed their tongues for pain, And blasphemed the God of heaven because of their pains and their sores, and repented not of their deeds. (Rev. 16:10, 11)

The Greek word used there for "darkness" means "to obscure or blind; to be full of darkness."[4] It suggests a darkness as thick as that in the silver mine, as we saw in Chapter 6. This darkness results from unbelief and rebellion, from an absence of light, as Paul describes in Ephesians 4:18, "Having the understanding darkened, being alienated from the life of God through the ignorance that is in them, because of the blindness of their heart."

However, all is not lost. Just as the Light broke forth to shatter the darkness in the beginning, as we saw in Genesis 1:3-4, so even during this terrible time of judgment, light will break forth. There is a popular saying of many Christians that is often posted as a meme on Facebook: "All the forces of darkness cannot stop what God has ordained."

This gem of wisdom comes from a verse in Isaiah: "For the LORD of Hosts has purposed, and who shall disannul it? And His hand is stretched out, and who shall turn it back?" (Isa. 14:27 MEV). The God of Creation cannot be destroyed. His purpose cannot be thwarted. His plan cannot be stopped. So, the Light will break forth and shatter the darkness again.

We must look to the final chapters of the Bible to see when this reality will come. And these chapters agree with Old Testament prophecies such as Daniel 7. Look at Daniel 7:9-14 in particular. What ends the terrible time of darkness, the tribulation, is the return of Jesus to set up the millennial kingdom, the time when Israel will rule over the nations.[5]

This return is pictured symbolically in Revelation 19:11-16, as Christ and the raptured saints riding horses (symbol of power). Jude, in verses 14-15, tells us about Enoch and the end times: "And Enoch also, the seventh from Adam, prophesied of these, saying,

'Behold, the Lord cometh with ten thousands of his saints, To execute judgment upon all . . . that are ungodly.'"

In Hebrews 11:5, Paul lists Enoch as one of the heroes of faith, and tells that he was translated without dying. We see Enoch's life in Genesis 5:18, 21-24. We can only surmise that when Enoch walked with God, in the light, God revealed to him these future events.

As the battle of Armageddon unfolds as seen in Revelation 19:17-21, all enemies of Israel and of God will be slain and become food for the birds of prey. Why would a good and loving God do this? Remember, He gave plenty of opportunity to everyone to believe. He sent his Son to pay the price for our salvation and to shine as light throughout human history.

Those who did not want the light turned away into darkness of their own free will. They chose darkness, and their choice excludes them from the Kingdom of Light. Remember Jesus' words in John 3:19-20 concerning those who love darkness because of their evil deeds and who reject the light because by it their evil deeds are revealed.

Besides being a good and loving God, God is also holy and just. If those who choose sin were not ultimately punished and abolished, where is the justice in the sacrificial death of Jesus Christ? Where is the justice and reward for those who choose the Light of Christ? Where is the manifestation of the difference between good and evil, light and dark, right and wrong? There must be an ultimate judgment of sinners because God is holy, righteous, good, loving, and wise. He gives us every opportunity to choose him. He provided a way for us to enter his family, by grace through faith in Jesus, the True Light, who offers life to whosoever believes (John 1:12 and 3:16).

Over and over in the Bible the invitation is given, like in Isaiah 55:6-7:

> Seek the LORD while He may be found, Call upon Him while He is near. Let the wicked forsake his way, and the unrighteous man his thoughts; Let him return to the LORD, and He will have mercy on him; And to our God, For He will abundantly pardon. (NKJV)

Peter tells us that the Lord does not want any to perish but desires that all would repent (2 Peter 3:9). In Ezekiel 33:11, we read that the Lord has "no pleasure in the death of the wicked," but desires that the wicked "turn from his way and live."[6] And that is exactly what we've done, who were lifted from the pit of darkness to walk in light. We turned from our own way and let God lift us from the pit of darkness. Unfortunately for those who choose darkness and sin, when the time comes for judgment, that judgment will fall.

If we proceed in the book of Revelation, we see the triumph of Light, as it covers a thousand years and then shines into eternity. Reading Revelation 20:1-6, we see the devil placed in the bottomless pit (that same one he tried to get us to enter in Chapter 1) and shut up there for one thousand years. During that time, he cannot roam the earth, deceiving, tempting, and misleading people.

The "first resurrection," spoken of in verse 5 refers to the full ranks of resurrection of the believers, ending with those, primarily of Israel, who will be raised at the beginning of the millennial kingdom. They were not previously resurrected (raptured, translated) with the church ranks, which are seen in several places in Revelation. Believers who fully yielded to God are seen first, in Revelation 5:9-10. Then, in Revelation 7:13-17 we see believers in Christ throughout the church age who yielded in part. And in Revelation 14:1-5 we see a group of Jewish believers in Christ, who are wholly dedicated to him.

These church rank believers come with Jesus to end the rebellion and set up the kingdom. In 1 Corinthians 15:22-23, Paul says, "For as in Adam all die, even so in Christ shall all be made alive. But every man in his own order: Christ the firstfruits; afterward they that are Christ's at his coming." The Greek word used for "order" means "something orderly in arrangement (a troop); a series or succession; like military ranks."[7] This shows us that there will be various groups who are resurrected as glorified bodies at different times. In fact, it started when Jesus rose. Read 1 Thessalonians 4:14-18 and 1 Corinthians 15:51-53 for additional information about this.

The resurrection in Revelation 20 would include those believers who died during the tribulation and believers from Israel and Gentile nations who died before Christ was born and were not raised when Jesus was. In Matthew 27:52-53, we read of a miraculous event:

> And the graves were opened; and many [not all] bodies of the saints [believers] which slept [were dead] arose, and came out of the graves after His resurrection, and went into the holy city [Jerusalem], and appeared unto many.

Imagine the stir they would have caused!

That group ascended to heaven when Jesus did, forty days later, according to Acts 1:9-10. They were the "cloud," even as we see a "cloud of witnesses" in Hebrews 12:1. But the others who lived in the Old Testament times will be raised at the beginning of the millennial kingdom, as described in Revelation 20:6—"the first resurrection." The rest of the dead—the wicked dead—will not be raised until the end of that thousand year period, and they will face the second death, according to Revelation 20:12-15.

At the end of that time of peace that will last a thousand years, the devil will be let out of the pit to deceive the nations that only give lip service to God and to Israel. In one last attempt to overthrow the people of God and God himself, Satan will amass a global army to attack. But the battle will be short-lived. Read Revelation 20:7-9. After that, the devil will permanently lose his place, position, and power. He will be "cast into the lake of fire and brimstone, where the beast and the false prophet are, and shall be tormented day and night for ever and ever" (Rev. 20:10).

In Chapter 9, we saw that this lake of fire and brimstone (hell) was prepared "for the devil and his angels," according to Matthew 25:41. God doesn't desire to send people there, but those people who reject his Son will send themselves there. They are the ones "not found written in the book of life." Read Revelation 20:11-15. This is commonly called the "white throne judgment," and it is the last judgment to fall, the grand climax of the mega-story of God's grace.

We should read Revelation 21 and 22 in full, keeping in mind the highly symbolic nature of the language. Imagine being in John's shoes, seeing all this glorious light, the events described, and the multitudes of people in heaven. How could you describe it? John lived in the first century A.D. He couldn't even refer to a movie or television show, to graphic arts or imaging, or to literature that might describe the universe as we see it through the Hubel telescope.

In an epistle, Paul said that he had been caught up to heaven in a vision, in or out of his body, he didn't know, and heard words that were impossible for man to speak (2 Corinthians 12:4). In 1 Corinthians 2:9, Paul quotes Isaiah 64:4 in saying, "Eye has not seen, nor ear heard, nor have entered into the heart of man the things which God has prepared for those who love Him" (NKJV). Spiritually seen, these things are understandable only in terms of known physical relationships and places, and that's how John described them.

But let us focus on the presence of light. This awesome city, comprised of believers, has a light like a precious stone. Think of a glistening diamond and the way it disperses light. The source of the light is seen in Revelation 21:23: "And the city had no need of the sun, neither the moon, to shine in it: for the glory of God did lighten it, and the Lamb is the light thereof." It is light that shines on everyone in

God's large family (see verse 24). And "there shall be no night there" (Rev. 21:25). See also Isaiah 60:19-20.

The light that shone into the darkness in the beginning (Gen. 1:3-4) is the same true Light that entered the world as Jesus, the Son of God (John 1:1-9, 12). It is the same light that God "shined in our hearts, to give the light of the knowledge of the glory of God in the face of Jesus Christ" (2 Cor. 4:6). And that light is the Light that lightens heaven for all eternity. Revelation 22:5 concludes, "And there shall be no night there; and they need no candle, neither light of the sun; for the Lord God giveth them light: and they shall reign for ever and ever."

What a triumph of God! What a triumph of Light over darkness. God calls us into that light so that He may bless us and grace us to live and reign with Him forever in a place where darkness, such as we face in this life, can never enter.

Moreover, Jesus tells us that after that white throne judgment, when the unbelievers will be cast into the lake of fire, "Then shall the righteous shine forth as the sun in the kingdom of their Father" (Matt. 13:43). Daniel speaks of the reward to those who teach truth and win souls: "And they that be wise [teachers] shall shine as the brightness of the firmament; and they that turn many to righteousness as the stars for ever and ever" (Dan. 12:3).

Furthermore, Paul, in 1 Corinthians 15:41-42, describes the different degrees of light to be seen in the different ranks: "There is one glory of the sun, and another glory of the moon, and another glory of the stars: for one star differeth from another star in glory. So also is the resurrection of the dead." We who believe will be part of the light that shines in heaven, so that there is no need of candles, electric lightbulbs, or sun in the sky.

Back to our hypothetical person who almost dropped into the bottomless pit of devil-inspired cultural darkness, but who was gloriously lifted out when calling on the name of the Lord:

You struggle against the invisible walls of the pit. You can't climb out. You jump up and down, but you cannot gain the height you need to clear the opening of the pit. You want that light, but you cannot attain to it. Despair and desperation fill your mind and heart. But there is no way out. No way to get to that light, to that wonderful voice, to that promise of life.

You feel the darkness swirl around you like a vortex sucking you down. Your mind reels. You open your mouth to scream. Only a whisper comes out: "Jesus, rescue me."

Suddenly your feet are on a solid rock with solid ground all around you. Light enfolds you. Behind you there is only a shadow of the pit that was, but it has no pull on you now.

You step toward the light's source. You can see! Everything around you is clear. You draw in a deep breath of fresh air and sigh, "Thank you, Jesus."

Now you see only light around you. The light dispels shadows that try to form across your path. The light grows brighter each step of the way. And as you look at it, intensely, you are transported in time to a vision of eternity. There you dwell in that glorious light where not even a shadow of darkness appears.

You rejoice in the tasks you do, there, in the land where Light triumphs.

Discussion Questions

1. Does all this seem possible? Or does it seem like a "fairy tale" to you? Be honest with each other and yourself.

2. Do you understand why judgment must fall on those who reject Christ and thereby reject the Triune God? Do you think that is fair? Can God be unfair?

3. Do you see how you've come from the growing darkness and the pit to a wonderful, marvelous kingdom of light?

Personal Reflection

1. Where do you think you will spend eternity? Why?

2. Does eternity seem so far away as to not be worth thinking about now?

3. Do you realize that every moment of life is a gift from God and that we never know when our life may end? Does that thought bring fear or hope to your mind? Or both? After all, if you have a family, especially small children, you don't want to think about leaving them. But if we live with our eyes set on eternity, our present will be with purpose, commitment, and devotion. We will "live intentionally."

Verses to Consider

1. Read Genesis 18:25; Deuteronomy 32:4; 2 Chronicles 19:7; Job 8:3, 20; 34:12; and Psalm 58:11.

    (a) Do you see that God is indeed just in His judgment of evil?

    (b) How would believers know they were right if they did not have a reward or consequence different from that of unbelievers?

    (c) Do you trust God to do what is right?

2. Read 2 Peter 3:13; Isaiah 65:17; 66:22; Revelation 21:1, 5; and 2 Corinthians 5:17.

    (a) Second Corinthians 5:17 says that "all things are become new." Keeping in mind that God exists outside of time and that he sees the future as already having happened, would you say that the creation of a new heaven and new earth are part of what Jesus "finished" at Calvary? Why or why not?

    (b) Do you see that there will be earth dwellers and heaven dwellers throughout eternity, though it will be quite a different earth from this one?

    (c) How would you describe what you envision regarding this? Can you draw it?

3. Read Psalm 1.

    (a) Is "the counsel of the ungodly," "the way of the sinners," and "the seat of the scornful" an appropriate way to describe the ideas, deeds, and attitudes of our wayward culture?

    (b) Do you see that meditating in the "law" of God refers not to the Ten Commandments or other laws, but to the "law of love" which Jesus gave?

    (c) Verses 3 and 4 give a different analogy for what we discuss as light versus dark. Can you think of other analogies to contrast these two positions regarding God?

Triumph of Light

(d) Do you see how this psalm provides an overview to all the Scriptures we read in these chapters?

4. Read Psalms 4:6; 56:13; 89:15; Colossians 1:12; Micah 7:8; and 2 Samuel 22:29.

   (a) The first verse above asks God to lift up the light of his countenance upon us; the third one speaks of walking in the light of his countenance. Notice that the ones who are blessed are the people who know "the joyful sound." That joyful sound is symbolically the sound of the shofar for feast days, for worship, and for the arrival of the King. As we long to see him, the light he shines on us will brighten. Do you long for that light and for the arrival of the King of kings and Lord of lords?

   (b) What do the other verses mean to you, concerning light? What is the correlation between "the light of the living" and "the inheritance of the saints in light"?

   (c) When would a saved person "sit in darkness"? Think about the culture that surrounds us. Consider depression that has reached epidemic proportions in our culture. Who has promised to be light for us in those situations? Can he make us be light for others in those situations?

   (d) According to 1 Peter 2:9, we are called "out of darkness into his marvelous light." Answering that call makes us "people of God," as Peter writes in the following verse. Has this been your experience?

   (e) If not, would you like it to be? And if so, do you desire more of his light?

Endnotes

Chapter 2

1. Ravi Zacharias, *The End of Reason: A Response to the New Atheists*. (Grand Rapids: Zondervan, 2008), 55. All rights reserved. Used by permission.
2. Morgan Lee, "Christian Dating Culture (Part 1): Majority of Christian Singles Reject Idea of Waiting Until Marriage to Have Sex," *The Christian Post* online, https://www.Christianpost.com/news/christian-dating-culture-part-1-majority-of-single-christians-reject-idea-of-waiting-for-marriage-to-have-sex-114422/, Feb. 12, 2014. Retrieved 30 June 2018. All rights reserved. Used by permission.
3. Taken from *Loving God with All Your Mind: Thinking as a Christian in the Postmodern World*, rev. ed. by Gene Edward Veith, Jr., Original Edition © 1987, Revised Edition © 2003, pp. 88-89. Used by permission of Crossway, a publishing ministry of Good News Publishers, Wheaton, IL 60187, www.crossway.org.

Chapter 4

1. Charles Montaldo, "Profile of Child Killer Susan Smith: The Tragic South Carolina Case of Murders of Michael and Alexander Smith." *ThoughtCo,* last updated December 30, 2018. https://www.thoughtco.com/susan-smith-profile-of-child-killer-972686.
2. Alpert Medical School of Brown University analysis of FBI's SHR data, qtd. in Criss, Doug, "A parent killing a child happens more often than we think," CNN online, Turner Broadcasting System, Inc., July 7, 2017. https://www.cnn.com/2017/07/07/health/

filicide-parents-killing-kids-stats-trnd/index.html, last modified July 7, 2017.
3. List of books: Please note that some of these are outdated and may have newer revised versions. At least one appears to be indie published, as publisher is not available.

The Case for a Creator: A Journalist Investigates Scientific Evidence That Points Toward God, Lee Strobel. Grand Rapids: Zondervan, 2004.

Deliver Us From Evolution: A Christian Biologist's In-Depth Look at the Evidence Reveals A Surprising Harmony Between Science and God. Aaron R. Yilmaz. 2016. (Also in e-book format.)

The Fingerprint of God: Recent Scientific Discoveries Reveal the Unmistakable Identity of the Creator. Hugh Ross. 2nd ed, Orange, CA: Promise Publishing Co., 1991; newer version available by Whitaker House, 2000.

What is Creation Science? Henry M. Morris and Gary E. Parker. El Cajon, CA: Master Books, 1987; Nineteenth printing available, July 2004.

Genesis and the Big Bang: The Discovery of Harmony Between Modern Science and the Bible. Gerald L. Schroeder, Ph., D. New York: Bantam, 1990.

The Great Divide: Christianity or Evolution? Gerard Berghoef and Lester Dekoster. Southampton, UK: Camelot Press, 1989.

The Illustrated Origins Answer Book: Concise, Easy-to-Understand Facts about the Origin of Life, Man, and the Cosmos. Paul S. Taylor. 4th ed. Mesa: Eden Productions, 1992.

Darwin's Doubt: The Explosive Origin of Animal Life and the Case for Intelligent Design. Stephen C. Meyer. New York: HarperCollins, 2014.

4. Hoyle, Fred and Nichandra Wickramasinghe. *Evolution from Space.* London: J. M. Dent & Sons, 1981, qtd. in *science forums.net, What Are the Odds of Life Evolving by Chance Alone?* Alan McDougall, "DNA Molecules and the Odds Against Evolution," July 22, 2012, last modified July, 2017. https://www.scienceforums.net/topic/67884-what-are-the-odds-of-life-evolving-by-chance-alone/. All rights reserved. Used by permission.

5. Alan McDougall, "DNA Molecules and the Odds Against Evolution," July 22, 2012, *science forums.net, What Are the Odds of Life Evolving by Chance Alone?* Last modified July, 2017. https://www.scienceforums.net/topic/67884-what-are-the-odds-of-life-evolving-by-chance-alone/. All rights reserved. Used by permission.

6. George Wald, "The Origin of Life," *Scientific American*, 191:48, May 1954 qtd. in "Evidence for Intelligent Design," *All About the Journey*, by AllAboutGod.com. Last modified May 1, 2019. https://www.allaboutthejourney.org/evidence-for-intelligent-design.htm. Copyright © 2002-2019. All About God Ministries, Inc. All rights reserved. Used by permission.

7. I. L. Cohen, *Darwin Was Wrong: A Study in Probabilities*, New Research Publications Inc., 1984, 6-7, qtd. in *All About the Journey*, by AllAboutGod.com. Aug. 8, 2018. https://www.allaboutthejourney.org/philosophy-of-life.htm. Copyright © 2002-2019. All About God Ministries, Inc. All rights reserved. Used by permission.

8. Ibid.

Chapter 5

1. Center for Disease Control and Prevention. National Center for Health Statistics, *National Vital Statistics Reports*, "Births: Final Data for 2017," Vol. 67, N. 8, November 7, 2018, last modified

March 31, 2017, https://www.cdc.gov/nchs/data/nvsr/nvsr67/nvsr67_08-508.pdf, at https://www.cdc.gov/nchs/fastats/unmarried-childbearing.htm.
2. Ravi Zacharias, "Flirting with the Truth, Part 2 of 4," *Just Thinking* radio broadcast, Jan. 23, 2018. Available at https://www.rzim.org/listen/just-thinking/flirting-with-the-truth-part-2-of-4. Ravi Zacharias International Ministries, Atlanta, GA. All rights reserved. Used by permission.

Chapter 6

1. "Gay," *Laird and Lee's Webster's New Standard Dictionary of the English Language: Students' Common School Edition* (Chicago: Laird and Lee, 1908), 222.
2. "Tolerance," Ibid., 611.
3. "Toleration," Ibid.
4. "Tolerance," *The Winston Simplified Dictionary: Encyclopedic Edition*, (Philadelphia: John C. Winston, 1931), 1048.
5. "Tolerance," *The New Lexicon Webster's Encyclopedic Dictionary of the English Language: Deluxe Edition*, (New York: Lexicon, 1991), 1038. All rights reserved. Used by permission.
6. "Tolerance," *Merriam Webster's Deluxe Dictionary: Tenth Collegiate Edition,* (Pleasantville: Reader's Digest, 1998), 1942.
7. "Tolerance," *Dictionary.com*. https://www.dictionary.com/browse/tolerance. All rights reserved. Used by permission.
8. "Tolerance," *The Wordsworth Concise English Dictionary*, (Hertfordshire: Wordsworth Editions Ltd., 1993), 564.
9. "Bioluminescence," *The New Lexicon Webster's Encyclopedic Dictionary of the English Language, Deluxe Edition*, (New York: Lexicon, 1991), 98.

Chapter 7

1. "Two New Children's Cartoon's [sic] to Be About Cross Dressing Drag Queens," June 13, 2018. Movieguide online, https://movieguide.org/news-articles/two-new-childrens-cartoons-to-be-about-cross-dressing-drag-queens.html.
2. Eric Teetsel, "Drag Queen Story Hour—Coming Soon!" September 6, 2018. Family Policy Alliance of Kansas, https://familypolicyalliance.com/issues/2018/09/06/drag-queen-story-hour-coming-soon.
3. Ibid.
4. *The Interlinear Greek-English New Testament*, Vol. IV of *The Interlinear Hebrew-Greek-English Bible*, Jay P. Green, Sr., General Editor and Translator, 2nd Ed., (Peabody: Hendrickson Publishers, 1985). All rights reserved. Used by permission. My modifications are in parentheses, as noted in the text.
5. Abort73.com. "Facts about Abortion: Abortion Statistics," last modified May 20, 2019, Loxafamosity Ministries, http://www.abort73.com/abortion_facts/us_abortion_statistics/. All rights reserved. Used by permission.

Chapter 8

1. Taken from *Loving God with All Your Mind: Thinking as a Christian in the Postmodern World*, rev. ed. by Gene Edward Veith, Jr., Original Edition © 1987, Revised Edition © 2003, pp. 88-89. Used by permission of Crossway, a publishing ministry of Good News Publishers, Wheaton, IL 60187, www.crossway.org.
2. Katie Pavlich, "Disgrace: Green Beret Who Defended Boy Against Rape in Afghanistan Loses Appeal," *Townhall*, September 23, 2015. townhall.com/tipsheet/katiepavlich/2015/09/23/army-to-green-beret-punished-for-defending-boy-from-an-afghan-rapist-nope-you-cant-come-back-n2055822.

3. Joseph Goldstein, "U.S. Soldiers Told to Ignore Sexual Abuse of Boys by Afghan Allies," *New York Times*, September 20, 2015. nytimes.com/2015/09/21/world/asia/us-soldiers-told-to-ignore-afghan-allies-abuse-of-boys.html.
4. Brandon Showalter, "Witches Outnumber Presbyterians in the US; Wicca, Paganism Growing 'Astronomically,'" October 10, 2018, *The Christian Post* online. https://www.christianpost.com/news/witches-outnumber-presbyterians-in-the-us-wicca-paganism-growing-astronomically-227857/. All rights reserved. Used by permission.
5. Massimo Introvigne, "The rise and rise of Wicca," December 5, 2018, *MercatorNet* online newsletter. https://mercatornet.com/above/view/the-rise-and-rise-of-wicca/22002.

Chapter 9

1. From Jay P. Green, Sr., General Editor and Translator, Vol. 3, *The Interlinear Hebrew-Greek-English Bible*, Peabody, MA: Hendrickson Publishers, 1984, p. 1693, along with a note from the *KJV* by Thomas Nelson regarding phrase "opened not the house of his prisoners" as literally meaning "did not let his prisoners loose homewards." All rights reserved. Used by permission.

Chapter 10

1. Author paraphrase of Psalm 40:12-13.
2. See Joel 2:32; Acts 2:21; and Romans 10:13.
3. Common quote by C. S. Lewis from his essay "Is Theology Poetry?" in the collection *The Weight of Glory,* qtd. in Goodreads.com, last modified with © 2019 Goodreads, Inc., https://www.goodreads.com/quotes/660-i-believe-in-christianity-as-i-believe-that-the-sun.

Chapter 11

1. See Colossians 3:17, 23-24 for two tests of God's will—acting in Jesus' name and doing it heartily as unto him. What follows is the reward of the inheritance.
2. Paraphrase utilizes margin notes from several study Bibles, the Hebrew-English Interlinear text, and Strong's *Concordance,* for Hebrew word meanings. The Interlinear text used is that of Jay P. Green, Sr., General Editor and Translator, Vol. 2, *The Interlinear Hebrew-Greek-English Bible*, Peabody: Hendrickson Publishers, 1984. All rights reserved. Used by permission.

Chapter 12

1. "Tribulation" as a specific event is mentioned in Matthew 24:21, 29; Mark 13:24; and Revelation 7:14. It is also mentioned as a general time of testing in various other verses.
2. Job 21:30; Zephaniah 1:15, 18; and Romans 2:5, among others.
3. Greg Laurie, "Forgiven and Free" sermon, Harvest Southern California, 19 Aug. 2018, online and televised on TBN.
4. Taken from *The New Strong's Exhaustive Concordance of the Bible* by James Strong, LL.D., S.T.D. Copyright © 1990 by Thomas Nelson Publishers. Used by permission of Thomas Nelson. www.thomasnelson.com.
5. Isaiah 60:1-3, 10-14; 61:4-9; 62:1-4; Ezekiel 36:24-30, 36-38; Revelation 21:24; Matthew 19:28; and Luke 22:29-30, among other verses. These show the promise to Israel to reign in the Millennial Kingdom. Other verses show that the church will assist Christ in ruling from heaven over the earth. See Romans 8:17; 2 Timothy 2:12; and 1 Corinthians 6:2-3. It is clear from the Greek-English Interlinear and the meaning of the Greek words that "we shall reign *over* the earth" (Rev. 5:10). Reigning *over* the earth is another subject, one that bears a thorough study though we haven't time here.

6. See also Ezekiel 18:23, 32.
7. Taken from *The New Strong's Exhaustive Concordance of the Bible* by James Strong, LL.D., S.T.D. Copyright © 1990 by Thomas Nelson Publishers. Used by permission of Thomas Nelson. www.thomasnelson.com.

Bibliography

Abort73.com. "Facts about Abortion: Abortion Statistics." Loxafamosity Ministries, Inc. Last modified May 20, 2019. http://www.abort73.com/abortion_facts/us_abortion_statistics/.

Center for Disease Control and Prevention. National Center for Health Statistics. *National Vital Statistics Reports.* "Births: Final Data for 2017." Last modified March 31, 2017. https://www.cdc.gov/nchs/data/nvsr/nvsr67/nvsr67_08-508.pdf at CDC website, https://www.cdc. gov/nchs/fastats/unmarried-childbearing.htm.

Cohen, I. L. *Darwin Was Wrong: A Study in Probabilities*, New Research Publications Inc., 1984, 6-7, qtd. in "Philosophy of Life," *All About the Journey*, website by *All About GOD Ministries, Inc.* Last modified August 8, 2018. https://www.allaboutthejourney.org/philosophy-of-life.htm Copyright © 2002-2019.

Criss, Doug. "A parent killing a child happens more often than we think." *CNN* online. Turner Broadcasting System, Inc. https://www.cnn.com/2017/07/07/health/filicide-parents-killing-kids-stats-trnd/index.html. Last modified July 7, 2017.

Dictionary.com, LLC. Last updated July 26, 2019. https://www.dictionary.com/.

Goldstein, Joseph. "U.S. Soldiers Told to Ignore Sexual Abuse of Boys by Afghan Allies." *New York Times*, September 20, 2015. nytimes.com/2015/09/21/world/asia/us-soldiers-told-to-ignore-afghan-allies-abuse-of-boys.html.

Green, Jay P., Sr., ed. and trans. *The Interlinear Hebrew-Greek-English Bible*, 2nd Ed. Vols. 1-4. Peabody: Hendrickson, 1985.

Hoyle, Fred and Nichandra Wickramasinghe. *Evolution from Space.* London: J. M. Dent & Sons, 1981. Qtd. in *science forums.net*,

What Are the Odds of Life Evolving by Chance Alone? Alan McDougall, "DNA Molecules and the Odds Against Evolution." July 22, 2012. Last modified July, 2017. https://www.scienceforums.net/topic/67884-what-are-the-odds-of-life-evolving-by-chance-alone/.

Introvigne, Massimo. "The rise and rise of Wicca," *MercatorNet* online newsletter, December 5, 2018. https://mercatornet.com/above/view/the-rise-and-rise-of-wicca/22002.

Laird and Lee's Webster's New Standard Dictionary of the English Language: Students' Common School Edition. Chicago: Laird and Lee, 1908.

Laurie, Greg. "Forgiven and Free." Sermon. *Harvest Southern California*. TBN and online. August 19, 2018.

Lee, Morgan. "Christian Dating Culture (Part 1): Majority of Christian Singles Reject Idea of Waiting Until Marriage to Have Sex." *The Christian Post* online. February 12, 2014. https://www.christianpost.com/news/christian-dating-culture-part-1-majority-of-single-christians-reject-idea-of-waiting-for-marriage-to-have-sex-114422/.

Lewis, C. S. "Is Theology Poetry?" *The Weight of Glory.* Qtd. in Goodreads.com. Last modified © 2019 Goodreads, Inc. https://www.goodreads.com/quotes/660-i-believe-in-christianity-as-i-believe-that-the-sun.

Lewis, William Dodge, Henry Seidel Canby, and Thomas Kite Brown, Eds. *The Winston Simplified Dictionary: Encyclopedic Edition.* Philadelphia: John C. Winston Co., 1931.

McDougall, Alan. "DNA Molecules and the Odds Against Evolution." July 22, 2012. *Science forums.net, What Are the Odds of Life Evolving by Chance Alone?* Last modified July, 2017. https://www.scienceforums.net/topic/67884-what-are-the-odds-of-life-evolving-by-chance-alone/.

Merriam-Webster's Deluxe Dictionary: Tenth Collegiate Edition. Pleasantville: Reader's Digest, 1998.

Bibliography

Montaldo, Charles. "Profile of Child Killer Susan Smith: The Tragic South Carolina Case of Murders of Michael and Alexander Smith." *ThoughtCo*. Last updated December 30, 2018. https://www.thoughtco.com/susan-smith-profile-of-child-killer-972686.

Movieguide online. "Two New Children's Cartoon's [sic] to Be About Cross Dressing Drag Queens." June 13, 2018. movieguide.org/news-articles/two-new-childrens-cartoons-to-be-about-cross-dressing-drag-queens.html.

The New Lexicon Webster's Encyclopedic Dictionary of the English Language: Deluxe Edition. New York: Lexicon, 1991. © 1990.

Pavlich, Katie. "Disgrace: Green Beret Who Defended Boy Against Rape in Afghanistan Loses Appeal." *Townhall,* September 23, 2015. townhall.com/tipsheet/katiepavlich/2015/09/23/army-to-green-beret-punished-for-defending-boy-from-an-afghan-rapist-nope-you-cant-come-back-n2055822.

Showalter, Brandon. "Witches Outnumber Presbyterians in the US; Wicca, Paganism Growing 'Astronomically.'" *The Christian Post* online. October 10, 2018. https://www.christianpost.com/news/witches-outnumber-presbyteri-ans-in-the-us-wicca-paganism-growing-astronomically-227857/.

Strong, James. *The New Strong's Exhaustive Concordance of the Bible.* Nashville: Thomas Nelson, 1990.

Teetsel, Eric. "Drag Queen Story Hour—Coming Soon!" September 6, 2018. Family Policy Alliance of Kansas. https://familypolicyalliance.com/issues/2018/09/06/drag-queen-story-hour-coming-soon.

Veith, Gene Edward, Jr. *Loving God with All Your Mind: Thinking as a Christian in the Postmodern World*, rev. ed. Wheaton: Crossway Books, 2003.

Wald, George. "The Origin of Life." *Scientific American*, 191:48, May 1954. Qtd. in *All About the Journey.* "Evidence for Intelligent Design." AllAboutGod.com. Last modified May 1,

2019. https://www.allaboutthejourney.org/evidence-for-intelligent-design.htm. Copyright © 2002-2019. All About God Ministries, Inc.

The Wordsworth Concise English Dictionary: Wordsworth Reference Ed. Hertfordshire: Wordsworth Editions Ltd., Chambers Harrap Publishers Ltd, 1993.

Zacharias, Ravi. *The End of Reason: A Response to the New Atheists*. Grand Rapids: Zondervan, 2008.

———. "Flirting with the Truth, Part 2 of 4," *Just Thinking* radio broadcast, Jan. 23, 2018.

Suggested Reading

Armed for Battle: A Balanced Approach to Spiritual Warfare by Peter N. Lundell, Beacon Hill Press, 2001.

Brainwashed: How Universities Indoctrinate America's Youth by Ben Shapiro, WND Books, 2004.

Cry Mercy: America's One Hope May Be in Her Destruction by M. K. Gantt, Logos Publications, 2018.

Cry Repent: Can the Church Find Its Voice Again? by M. K. Gantt, mkgantt.com Publications, 2019.

Culture Shock: A Biblical Response to Today's Most Divisive Issues by Chip Ingram, Baker Books, 2014.

Dark Agenda: The War to Destroy Christian America by David Horowitz, Humanix Books, 2018.

Deliver Us from Evil: Restoring the Soul in a Disintegrating Culture by Ravi Zacharias, Word Publishing, 1996.

Destroying the Shadow Agenda: A Christian Manifesto by Bruce Porter, Liberty Trades, LLC, 2019.

The End of Reason: A Response to the New Atheists by Ravi Zacharias, Zondervan, 2008.

Loving God with All Your Mind: Thinking as a Christian in the Postmodern World by Gene Edward Veith, Jr., (Rev. ed.), Crossway Books, 2003.

The New Absolutes: How They Are Being Imposed on Us, How They Are Eroding Our Moral Landscape, by William D. Watkins, Bethany House, 1996. (This book is out of print, but stay alert for a new book by Watkins dealing with the topic.)

Prayer Power: 30 Days to a Stronger Connection with God by Peter Lundell, Revell, Baker Publishing Group, 2009.

About the Author

A born-again Christian, Victoria is an ordained pastor who speaks and teaches at local churches and writes Bible studies. She has taught college level composition and literature classes to both traditional and non-traditional students, substituted in several schools, and has worked in both public and private accounting as a former CPA.

She has written award-winning screenplays and has published two other books using pen names, a novel, *Out of the Prison House* (V. D. Carroll), and a collection of literary poetry, *Angel Unaware: Poems* (Victoria Carroll).

This book is the first in a planned set of three books to discover and share the power of the True Light—our Lord Jesus Christ. The topic has burned in Victoria's heart for over five years as our culture has darkened considerably. Our nation's celebration of sin, under the guise of progressivism and political correctness, threatens to destroy even the strongest denominations in this country. Indeed, we are set as lights "in the midst of a crooked and perverse nation" (Phil. 2:15).

You can learn more about Victoria on her website, where you can subscribe to her blog. You will be able to receive emails with free Bible studies, information about new books as they become available, and news about Victoria's other endeavors. See more at VictoryThroughLight.com.

Dear reader,

If you found this book illuminating and helpful, I invite you to write a review on Amazon.com or another site. It helps me know how I can better serve my readers as I share the light of the gospel of Jesus Christ.

I also welcome you to visit my ministry website, VictoryThrough Light.com/. There you can access my blogs and other freebies. You will also find information about my writing and speaking ministry. My hope is that the site will encourage and empower you. You can also visit my author page on Facebook (https://fb.me/VictoriaDorshornAuthor).

My goal is to share the truth that no matter what foe or trial we face, we can be transformed from victim to victor through faith in Jesus Christ. Furthermore, we can confront the growing cultural darkness and overcome its influence on our lives, our relationships, and our society.

If you are interested in having me come and speak, please email me at vdorshorn@gmail.com or call 785-727-0369.

Feel free to contact me with questions or feedback. I would love to hear your thoughts about the growing cultural darkness and how it affects your life, and even more importantly, how the True Light of Jesus has empowered you for victorious living. You may email me at vdorshorn@gmail.com.

In Christ, Victoria Dorshorn

Available through Amazon.com, BarnesandNoble.com,
or other book outlets in print or ebook.

Quantity discounts for your small group or Sunday School class.
Email vdorshorn@gmail.com.

www.ingramcontent.com/pod-product-compliance
Lightning Source LLC
Chambersburg PA
CBHW020532080526
44583CB00013B/833